TABLE OF CONTENTS

EXECUTIVE SUMMARY

American society has undergone a series of "transformations" that come in five forms: The white man is the new demi-god. The white woman is the new white man. The black man is the new gay. The black woman is the new black man (A combination of machismo and lesbianism). The gay is the new "nigga." This is what I see and this book will explain it to you and provide evidence. Sex roles and perceptions are changing and as a result, so are power relationships.

INTRODUCTION

The question is, what is all this shit about being afraid of women and doing things when they are not present that you wouldn't do if they were there? It's a changing of the guard and men, because of the laws and because of her independence, have become afraid of women. But in my view there is more taking place than meets the eye. There's a "transformation" taking place and it's about time somebody did more than just laugh about the possibility of what is taking place.

Roles are changing and shifting, and not just in terms of endogamy, exogamy, hypogamy or hypergamy. The roles I am talking about are incredibly significant because they transcend sex role socialization, but are about essential sex roles themselves and the sociopolitical roles and obligations that come with them: in sum, the white woman is the new white man, the black woman is the new white woman, the black man is the new "gay" man, the homosexual is the new "nigga", and the white man is, indeed, the new deity (demi-god). Following are explanations and evidence of why I believe each of these to be the case

Television as Inter-Cultural Engineer

When you turn on television in the morning and see blonde Kelly Ripa and giant African-American Michael Strahan, you begin the illusion that America is changing. Add that to the fact that the President of the United States is in his second term, and the fantasy broadens.

The question is: why Strahan and what is the strategy here?

CHAPTER 1:
The Black Woman as Machismo/
The Rise of the "Sister Dyke"

Back in the 1960s, this white senator named Daniel Patrick Moynihan labeled the black family a "matriarchy." He said that it was run and dominated by the woman, and Black scholars, including myself, dogged the shit out of him and basically pawned it off as racism. But the system worked to make this statement come to pass: Since the 1960s it is the black man who has been shot down by cops and arrested in huge numbers and placed in prisons. A large number of them have come out of the closet and of course, want nothing to do with a female. This has left the black family in the hands of the black woman who, for the most part, already thought she was in charge. Now it has REALLY gone to her head.

Hence my name for this hybrid female: the "sister-dyke." This is the sister-dyke: not necessarily fucking other women, but assuming the role traditionally held by and attributed to that of an aggressive male when things get tough.

How else to explain these women walking up on football sized men and taking swings at them? How else to explain women slapping men so hard that it sounds like a shot was fired? How else to explain some of the insults and curses hurled by these women at men, women and children when they become angered? This comes from the transformation that I am alleging exists: the black woman is the new super-dyke stereotype. And I'm going to prove it.

I believe that when it comes to the Black family, what appears to be a patriarchy is really a lesbian-oriented matriarchy (either overtly or covertly). An article titled, "Patriarchy," by Allan Johnson (printed in In Paula S. Rothberg (Ed.) Race, Class and Gender in the United States. New York: Worth Publishers. 2001.) provides information that I will now flip to show that what I say about these "transformed sister-dykes and their "power" rings true.

I believe that Johnson's article, written in 1997, had two major points . The first appears on page 133 where he writes,

> Because patriarchy is male-identified and male-centered,
> women and the work they do tends to be devalued, if not
> made invisible. In their industrial capitalist form, for
> example, patriarchal cultures do not define the unpaid
> domestic work that women do as real work, and if women
> do something, it tends to be valued less than when men do
> it."

Using the concepts of "male-identified" and "male-centered" as the nexus for the reminder of the article, Johnson then begins to touch upon issues that are obvious, and yet eye opening. For instance, he writes that, "If you want a story about heroism, moral courage, spiritual transformation, endurance, or any of the struggles that give human life its deepest meaning and significance, men and masculinity are usually the terms in which you must see it ... Male experience is what patriarchal culture offers to represent HUMAN experience and the enduring themes of life, even when these are most often about women in the actual living of them ... " (p. 132.)

But when it comes to today's black community, especially the majority which is locked into the urban core, and when what was just written is flipped and applied to the new single head of household, the new Black female -- the sister-dyke. She wants to be viewed as a white woman by whites, wanted to assume the role of "boss" when it comes to Black men, and wants to be viewed as the shot-caller for the black community when it comes to responses by white decision makers. She wants to be both loved and feared – much like a Mafioso boss.

This is so true. Even in the study of African-American and African history, the women are usually mentioned either only in passing, or they are women who assumed courageous roles, in other words, roles that most people would assign to males. But they assumed masculine approaches to fighting the system. We have Harriet Tubman and Sojourner Truth, for example: two women who dealt with the system in different ways, but who are cited because of their appeal to men: Harriet Tubman because she showed extraordinary courage in leading the enslaved out of bondage, and Sojourner Truth because she appealed to the patriarchal system and was therefore invite to meet the president of the United States. You can add Ida B. Wells to that list.

Now lets' take the previous paragraph and better understand how the "sister-dyke" is now the norm when it comes to the black community.

The new black community, riddled and torn up by racist cops, illegal arrests, drug abuse, teen pregnancy, gang domination, mass incarceration and black on black homicide, is now run by women. In addition, Black men because of our actions, are viewed as docile derelicts. So to re-write the first sentence of the previous paragraph, we have this: "Because the sister-dyke is female-identified but male-centered, men and the activities they engage in tend to be devalued, if not made invisible. The sister-dyke has largely learned to ignore the Black man, except on an "as need" basis (e.g., rent money, an escort for a social gathering of some kind, child support, occasional sexual trysts, getting their "hair done," pocket money, etc.).

There is also a racial twist when we flip the previous words by Johnson. Today's reality would go something like this: "In their industrial capitalist form, for example, sister-dyke communities do not define the unpaid relationship work that men do as real work, and if men do something, it tends to be valued less than when women do it." See? The society we live in has deformed male-female relationships for everybody, but it is more evident and pervasive among us than it is among others. After all, as the saying goes, "when America has a cold, black folks have pneumonia."

Black female courage is nothing new. Kwame Nkrumah once wrote, "The degree of a country's revolutionary awareness may be measured by the political maturity of its women." And in black history, as I alluded to earlier, it was black women who were out there dealing daily. From sisters like Ida B. Wells and Mary McCleod-Bethune to Fannie Lou Hamer, Rosa Parks and Angela Davis, black women have been right there on the front lines of the struggle. The same is true in every single African struggle. But in the U.S. these women have become so frustrated, bitter and angry, they have re-defined themselves and their relationships. And the sister-dyke is what you get.

A second key point made in the article appears on page 135. Johnson writes,

> For women, gender oppression is linked to a cultural devaluing of femaleness itself. Women are subordinated and treated as inferior because they are culturally defined as inferior AS WOMEN, just as many racial and ethnic minorities are devalued simply because they aren't considered to be white. Men, however, do not suffer more because maleness is devalued as an oppressed status in relation to some higher, more powerful one (emphasis original).

Here's how the previous paragraph about "patriarchy" should read as it describes the status, style and substance of the "sister-dyke: "For the sister-dyke, gender oppression is linked to a cultural devaluing of both femaleness and blackness. Women, in general, are subordinated and treated as inferior because they are culturally defined as inferior. So they adopted a defensive formulation of toughness and self-defense. She is also angry because wearing her long extensions, makeup and using skin lightener still as yet doesn't enable her to be considered "acceptable" (white). Black Men, the new faggots, do not suffer more because their maleness is devalued as an oppressed status in relation to some higher, more powerful one. In fact, these Black men have abandoned and are now apparently redefining their maleness.

Dykes want other women as mates, but such a choice is socially unacceptable so some hide it. Even in this day and age, lesbians are frowned upon for the most part. These "girlfriend clubs" and "girls night out" bullshit you see going on: this is the hunting ground for the dyke. They are systematically adopting male roles and even male dress. They want to shake hands like the brothers, use the terminology of the brothers and so on because they both hate and admire us. They want that black male swagger because most of them feel they'll never find " a good man" because, as most of them think, "all men are dogs." So if you can't find a good man – then just BECOME one! As the character Hud said in the movie by the same name, "no use shooting the whole pack of dogs when only one has fleas." But you cannot convince these bitter and oftentimes abused black women of this.

We have always had sister-dykes in our midst. One source documents it:

> Although a number of lesbian and bisexual blues singers--
> including Bessie Smith, Ma Rainey, Josephine Baker, and
> Ethel Waters--attained a level of sexual openness in their
> music, these women generally hid their same-sex
> relationships behind a public guise of heterosexuality. Only
> rarely did their lyrics even allude to their sexual desire for
> other women, and generally all such allusions were tinged
> with an ambivalence suggesting an elusive sexuality …
> (GLBTQ, 2009).

Does knowing that Josephine Baker, Bessie Smith, Ethel Waters, or Ma Rainey were dykes make you appreciate them any less? Of course not. I'm just saying admit what you are, act it out so that I can tell, and then I know where that relationship is going to go. The social stigma was great, so they hid their desires from the public. But the fact still remains that too many sister-dykes are living a lie the way the sisters just mentioned had to do. In a patriarchal society, the sister-dyke is living a life of self-deception which, in turn, forces her to deceive others.

I have always believed that even the dirt poor white hillbilly could identify with someone like George Bush because both were white. But the male aspect is also a factor and Johnson explains that nicely on page 132:

> Since patriarchy identifies power with men, the vast majority of
> men who aren't powerful but are instead dominated by other
> men can still feel some connection with the IDEA of male
> dominance and with men who ARE powerful. It is far easier, for
> example, for an unemployed working-class man to identify with

> male leaders and their displays of patriarchal masculine
> toughness than it is for women of any class ... In this way male
> identification gives even the most lowly-placed man a cultural
> basis for feeling some sense of superiority over the otherwise
> most highly placed woman (which is why a construction worker
> can feel within his rights as a man when he sexually harasses a
> well-dressed professional woman who happens to walk by?)

But it is also this way for sister-dykes.

For instance, the previous paragraph about patriarchy would read like this when discussing the sister-dyke:

Since patriarchy identifies power with men, the vast majority of Black women who can't locate men and/or hate the men they can still feel some connection with the IDEA of male dominance by becoming "sister-dykes" and adopting the role of father and mother, protector, provider because they are tired of being used and dumped by men who they allowed into their lives. It is far easier, for example, for an employed working-class sister-dyke to identify with white male leaders (demi-gods) and their displays of patriarchal masculine toughness than it is for women of any class to accept a black male who is gradually turning into a faggot In this way male identification by the sister-dyke gives even the most lowly-placed Black woman a cultural basis for feeling some sense of superiority over the black man and other men of color.

The ranks of the sister-dyke are growing. Some call them lesbians, but there are a lot who are pretending to be in that life just so that they can have companionship and as a result, like most adult human beings, get a nut whenever they can. Just like many Black men are on the down low, black women have been sexing each other up for decades.

<u>Politics</u>

The sister-dyke can assume dual roles: that of slut that is male oriented or that which is dyke, where she can go after what she really wants: *pussy*. She's tired of sperm running down her leg as the man snores next to her, tired of the lack of pillow talk, tired of not getting head, tired of sucking foot long dick and ending up with a facial, tired of him thinking that cuddling is for sissies (a cover for the fact that he is really on the down low) and tired of him getting a quick nut and then disappearing out the door. She's tired of having to beg for massages or being touched "in that place" when, if she switches sides and gets a girlfriend, she won't have to worry about these things.

Put another way, following the white woman's historical example, the sister-dyke has learned how to use "pussy politics" to control her life in a number of ways and further, to use the white man's system to secure a lifestyle albeit an impoverished one. And it is this version of "pussy politics" that, to this day, dominates the "sister dyke's role as "family backbone" and aids and abets in the black man's assumptive role as effeminate. Let me explain.

To begin with there's the "I don't need no man" shit that the white woman started with her "Women's Liberation" movement. Other versions of the new liberated woman, which created the philosophy for the sister-dyke, can be found in statements regarding how silly a man is, how easy a man is to seduce, and how expendable they are include,"all a man is good for is a fuck," "if you're going fishing, you gotta use the right bait," and of course," If you get over one man get under another one," and "men are like buses: there's one coming down the street every hour." All of these are versions of "social and sexual independence" that white women feel and strive for, and now the black woman is following suit. The white woman adopts lesbianism out of choice; the black woman does it after a forced choice or necessity. For the sister-dyke, her dual role is one of survival.

The heyday for the black woman now turned quasi-dyke was the advent of the Blaxploitation movement, where movies and characters like, "Foxy Brown,' "Sheba, Baby," "Cleopatra Jones" and "Friday Foster" paved the way for the super fine, super independent woman who only associated with men when they could join her "team" and serve as her willing thralls. In those movies the sisters were large (sometimes literally) and in charge, and all men were asked to do was serve as sidekicks, flunkies and occasionally, a love interest. From there women started dressing for each other, going on in groups, dancing together and as you can see, it is considered "sexy" by some males (not me) to see two women making out with each other. The acceptance of the sister-dyke had arrived!

Today is much the same as black male numbers dwindle at an alarming rate and the belief that "all the good men are taken" or "there ain't no good black men" seems to dominate most of their thinking. Even when they hang out in clubs or lounges, they're basically in there looking for some money attached to a penis – when back in the day, it was the other way around. They're on the prowl at the club, at the supermarket, in the library, or even in church -- perhaps to set some brother up with a pregnancy, but only after they check his credit rating, driver's license and other identification like the white woman trained her to do.

They now have their own money, their own cars and in some cases, their own homes (sometimes left behind by a deceased husband or other family member). All they aspire for now is a serious relationship so that their girlfriends won't think they are dykes. They might even go so far as to get pregnant to stabilize their cover. But they know that they tread dangerous ground with their deception, so they need legal protection. That's where the spike in "domestic violence' comes in.

And it's working under the cover of male morality where these effeminate, downlow-oriented, metro males promote a philosophy of "never hit a woman" bullshit.

On the December 5, 2012 segment of "First Take," Stephen A. Smith – somewhat effeminate in his own right -- continued to drive home the fact that a man should *never put his hand on a woman*. But then he turned around and made some impactful statements about men having to "fall on their swords" and sometimes have to "admit to things they didn't do" in order to comply with society's standards so that they (the athletes) could continue to do their jobs and not fall out of public favor. Smith who boasts that he was "raised by five women" (as he did most recently during a September 8, 2015 segment of "First Take") is one more example of how the feminine view of reality can be imposed on a child – male or female. As I say, Smith is more effeminate than he may care to admit.

I say, "dawa na moto ni moto" -- fight fire with fire.

These women in general and the sister-dyke, in particular, are armed with weapons that are legal, social, cultural, political – and gender-biased, although the latter is usually shrouded and covered up by the white man's blatant and long-time sexism and glass ceiling-related antics. And all of these components fall under an ideological umbrella, basically a Euro-American one, that states that if you hit a woman there is going to be hell to pay. And the subtle and degrading message that women are willing to sell their souls for so that they can retain this power, is that they are "inferior and childlike" and therefore in need of this kind of "protection."

Remember: the white man views himself as a demi-god, all-powerful and therefore in charge of all things. Notice that when this society talks about "vulnerable groups," or when a ship, a burning building or a disaster has destroyed a given area is, the claim is always, "women and children first." On almost every single level women, no matter how dyke-like or hard core, are viewed as "things to be protected" and placed on the same level as kids. The emphasis is on "things" because that is just what they are being treated like: objects and commodities.

And in this society, what kind of women do men prefer when it comes to seeking a date or a mate? The ones that are the most weak minded, child-like, defenseless and dependent. But it's just a front: the sister-dyke might play possum during a date, but once the relationship is "safe" (e.g., with a pregnancy set up, a marriage proposal, etc.) she goes into that nurturing mode which increasingly becomes more and more dominant. And since the black man is slowly becoming more effeminate and bitch-like, the relationship flips: she wears the pants and makes the decisions, he wears the earrings, gets his hair done and when possible, takes it up the ass from the neighbors or his pals. This is taking place while she treats the male in the relationship like a child who can't even hold his own dick when he takes a piss.

The whites have a slogan in regard to their age: "I'm 50 years YOUNG" or whatever their age might happen to be. Everybody wants to be a child and that is why being treated like one comes too easy for so many. This is then followed up with another sexist mantra: the man's job is to "take care" of his family, and who does that consist of? Women and children. The sister-dyke goes so far as to use HIS paycheck to horde away a little money on the side (for "night clubbing purposes") and make sure the home is cared for. After the first few years he tires of her, stops fucking her, hides in his "man cave" which in turn, paves the way for three things: (1) a whole lot of jacking off and pornography viewing with the door locked, (2) the "downlow" with some of his equally effeminate pals, and (3) opportunities, for her, to date women (commonly known as "girl's night out")

Therefore, when it comes down to that "domestic abuse" bullshit, "fight fire with fire" is my contribution to making the situation far more equitable. It gives the female back her humanity. It lets her know that if she swings on me, I'm gonna swing on her. If she hits me, I'm going to hit her back. That makes it fair, and it shows that we are indeed, equal. If she has the nerve to take the risk of hitting someone that can retaliate, maybe she'll think twice. The argument about "well, you're a man and you're stronger," is precisely my point: she already knew that! Women are attracted to strength, which is why they seek to corral it and then control it. She sees me and knows what I can do! So knowing that, why would she take a swing at me or hit me in violence? Because she lost her temper? Because I made her mad? Because I didn't do what she told me to do? Fuck that!

But the real reason for her to take a swing is because she's a sister-dyke. She doesn't respect men because they are competing with her for pussy. She sees every man as the enemy, as quiet as it's kept. It's the politics of sexual differences, where women have the upper hand. All they have to do is lay there and they can get a nut. Even the most naïve and backward among them can become "a good lay" by just laying there and letting out fake screams of ecstasy. On the other hand, the male has to have boners, and that is as psychological as it is physical. Simply put, she can control our sex drive by bugging the shit out of us, creating a pressure-charged situation and generally turning us off. If not, then shower us with fake compliments about how good we are in bed and how our dick is the best they've ever had. They've been doing it for centuries, and the Black woman was in on it, too. But she could cook and dance, so dumb ass niggas that we are, we didn't see it coming.

If she knows that I can kick her ass, then she should take that into consideration before she has the nerve to try to kick mine! But the fact is, she knows she has the courts on her side and if things get bad, a divorce will get her half my shit. But she attacks because she doesn't respect your humanity and therefore she thinks she has a right to challenge it. She has no business trying to put her hands on an ex-street fighter and think that just because she has tits and a vagina that she won't get hit back.

That shit might work on the ignorant downlow niggas. But not on me.

Popular Culture

The sister-dyke is not just a status but also a role – Black women with the equivalent powers of a black man, doing the bidding of the white system. Although the white man still gives the ordered (being a demi-god and all), this new wave black woman has a masculine image and usually a high position – a position that no Black man would ever be entrusted with or assigned to.

For instance, there's "Scandal," which stars fine-ass Kerry Washington, and the plot is so unbelievable you have to ask yourself: whose dick did she suck to get this part? America is really going all out putting these black women in these prime time roles - anyone is better than a Black male (who white female viewers might find "attractive"). Witness, for instance, Taraji P. Henson in "Person of Interest" (killed off), Meagan Good in NBC's "Deception ," And "Sleepy Hollow" is filled with black women: the sister Abbie Mills appears to have a thing for the white boy Ichabod Crane, and then the woman who plays her sister, Jennie. Both shot guns, stab and slice demon s, fight monsters and so on.

The lone black man on the show, Captain Frank Irving, is played by Orlando Jones. And even though he's the police captain, nobody really respects and in many ways he comes off as the effeminate side piece. To add to his impotence is his ex-wife, who appears now and then to show him the pussy he'll never get again and brings his young daughter along to flash, just to egg him on more. In other words his role, like the roles of most black men in the lives of the sister-dyke (and society in general), is weak, second-rate, and limp. He's also another in a long line of police chiefs that no one listens to.

Why "women firsts" when it comes to bad situations? They want to be a male's equal, but they still expect their doors to be opened. You call it chivalry; I call it acting a damn fool.

For instance, merely look at the popular culture movies. Go back as far as 1939's "Five Came Back" (Lucille Ball, Chester Morris. Wendy Barrie) about a plane that is wrecked but of the 12 people who were on board, they have to decide which five can re-board because of the condition of the plane. "We have to consider women and children first," is the universal agreement. How about the movie, "Titanic"? The same thing was shouted after it hit the fateful iceberg: "women and children to the life boats first!"

Strong black women taking the place of black men. And as the new black men, look at how they are presented: no shuffling, no skinning and grinning, but in positions of power. They are the new black men only when working with and taking orders from, the white man. These women have juice, carry guns, seduce powerful white men and do battle with bad guys. Sister-dykes, one and all.

<u>Never Strike a Sister-Dyke</u>

A key reason why this society claims that a man should never strike a woman is because, first of, it reinforces the myth of the female being "the weaker sex." In other words, treat her the way you would treat a child, and believe me, throughout history, that is exactly how she's been treated. Even their own Bible says in Proverbs 23:13-14, ""Withhold not correction from a child: for if thou strike him with the rod, he shall not die. Thou shalt beat him with the rod, and deliver his soul from hell." (Proverbs 23:13-14). When it came to women though, the "rod" was the dick, and if you withheld it and only gave it during times of good behavior, you could control *her* behavior.

Not no mo'!

That is why so many of them, being under estimated, have been able to assume control of so much. From the myth of them being "weak" came the "morality plays" that are pawned off as television shows and movies, and the message that they convey. After watching these movies and programs, I've heard black women make statements like, "you're less than a man if you hit a woman." I've heard these dumb ass sportscasters and athletes say shit like, "You should never, ever hit a woman."

But the sister-dyke is smart: she can feign femininity when needed. That's why this chivalry directed toward those of her ilk is foolhardiness at best. And when she sees that some dunce (male) of the type that under estimated her because of her gender, she's thinking, "He fell for it." Let me explain with some examples.

My question, once again, is: how can such unsubstantiated bullshit about a human being, just because she has a vagina and breasts, last for so long and among so many different people in a nation as large as this one? It's all rooted in the male obsession with and apparent "need" for pussy. Sometimes even *she* must be shocked at what a man will do to get between her legs. Begging for dates, spending money on dinner, movies and concerts; diamond rings, watches and paying bills as the date is prolonged into a courtship. So she knows, beforehand, that her pussy has value. So she uses it the way people use something of value: *as a bargaining chip.*

Let me share a little story with you. When some Haitian immigrants moved into Miami back in the 1990s, they couldn't speak the language so the parents had their kids translate for them. The kids started seeing that this power to interpret shit carried a lot of power with it, so they started using that power to control the family.

It's the same way with pussy: the greater the cockhound the greater the power that these sister-dykes have over that hound. In more philosophical terms, "He who has the ability to satisfy human needs controls the humans that have those needs". Men, being the whoremongers that we are , can easily be controlled by pussy. It's been going on since before the days of Samson and Delilah.

Now for some contemporary examples.

Former pro football wide receiver Chad Johnson allegedly head butted his wife of five weeks Evelyn Lozada. She called the cops in a frantic fit, and Johnson went to jail for it. He also lost his job as wide receiver for the Miami Dolphins, a million dollar paycheck and got humiliated throughout the media. In fact, this bitch appeared on a number of television talk shows talking shit and playing "the wounded female." On December 5, 2012, Johnson appeared on ESPN's "First Take" and was continuing to beg and then shared with the audience that he was court-ordered "to enroll in and complete 26 weeks of anger management courses." This bitch has since remarried and probably got one hell of an alimony check.

What kind of bullshit is this? Do you know who this bitch Evelyn Lozada is? She is on the program, "Basketball Wives" which stars a bunch of bitches who you wouldn't know from Adam's house cat were it not for the fact that they were married to (or had kids by) current and former NBA players, including some players that really weren't even that great. At any rate, I saw Evelyn Lovado throw sand at her ex-husband (who threw a glass of water in her face), pull out a bottle to attack another black woman, call other black women bitches on a regular basis on camera, and basically show that she is just another fine, out-of-control bitch.

Chad Johnson comes along and talks her out of her panties, after all, he IS a pro athlete and the sister-dyke can get security and financial gain and when he's gone to practice or at away games, she can do whatever she wants -- with whichever gender she wants. As Mr. Smithers of "The Simpsons" would say, "Perfect, Simpson, perfect."

Johnson was taking her out on expensive dates and evidently "dick-whipping" her. She fell for him right away, and on one program one of her colleagues said she was a "ho" and that Johnson wouldn't be faithful because he was a ho, too. Evelyn went off again. So she marries Johnson and she finds out he's messing around with another woman because she found a condom in the trunk of his car.

Then, like most bitches who believe they've "landed a sucker" now that they've strolled down the aisle, she went through his car and his cell phone, and found just the "dirt" she was evidently looking for. This is what started the argument in the car which led to the head butt which he faced on-going public ridicule about. Co-host Stephen A. Smith of ESPN's "First Take" declared, "You don't put your hands on a woman, period!" Why? Because this effeminate asshole says so? This bitch didn't have any business trying to confront somebody and getting all up in that man's face, acting as if she was going to whip HIS ass! Chad Johnson was a professional football player. This bitch knew he had other women. Why is she acting as if she's so surprised?

Another case in point: What about this bitch Rihanna? Chris Brown's phone rings while they're in his car and he's behind the wheel. She snatches it to see who it is and they start arguing. She won't give him back his phone so he fires on her ass and it's on. She's fighting him and giving as good as she gets. Check out the lyrics to some of her songs, and you can see what kind of woman this is – those Caribbean bitches, like the Puerto Rican Evelyn Lozado, don't take that shit. This is the sister-dyke: not necessarily fucking other women, but assuming the role of a man when things get tough. If you're willing to mix it up, then be willing to take that ass whipping when you inevitably lose.

This society endorses the tough female and promotes it at all levels. They call it being assertive or aggressive, traits that any real man can handle. But these bitches, like most black people, can't handle real power when they get it. Haven't you noticed that more money Black people get, the greater their tendency to turn start getting into gay sex and other freaky shit that they never would have dreamed of when they were broke? Some may be just "sampling," but I don't believe in that shit. There is no such thing as bi-sexuality or being "bi-curious": if you're a woman, you either like dick or you like another woman's tongue and a 12-inch dildo in your pussy. Choose one and stick with it!

There's an old saying in the black community: "Fair exchange ain't no robbery." That basically means when its tit for tat, things are even. Where is the fair exchange when it comes to men and women and physical abuse? If and when guys do it, or even hit a woman, it's straight to jail, do not pass go, do not collect $200. When a woman does it, she can get away with it if she cries hard enough, lies good enough, and if she calls the cops fast enough. I, for one, don't see anything "fair" about this kind of 'exchange.'

<u>Popular Culture</u>

Popular culture serves to buttress the politics of the sister-dyke.

In a society where pussy is craved and sought out like the ore of the Gold Rush of the 1800s, craving booty was a male domain. Having seen that, women have flipped the script and upped the ante: since it appears that men want it so bad, they must now **pay for it unlike any other time in history**. Not only with money, which is why prostitution is the world's oldest profession, but with a secure lifestyle and blind obedience that begins with something called "the date."

I'm writing about the American version. Although dating is probably universal in European culture (which this society is based on), Americans have added their own twists and modifications to turn it into a romance-laden, capitalist extravaganza. And whatever the white man does for and toward his mate, the black woman sees it and turns around and manipulates the black man, in his quest for pussy, *to do the same thing to and for her.*

Steve Wilkos, former protégé of Springer, now has his own show, "The Steve Wilkos Show." He uses a direct and confrontative approach but even with security guards on stage, there have been a number of programs where the woman, standing directly in front of the man and with Wilkos watching, has been allowed to slither past the guards and knock the shit out of a man. These women are allowed to hit and paw at men. No man is allowed to retaliate or, no matter what the controversy, ever get physical. His wife is one of the executive producers.

On the October 5, 2012 segment of "The Steve Wilkos Show," he's trying to offer advice to these two lesbians who are in a relationship. One of them "puts her hands" on the other on a regular basis. Wilkos shares that in his marriage, "If I go home and slap my wife, she's gone. She's not going to give me a second chance." He said even before they got into the marriage it was agreed that, "If you put your hands on me, it's over." I doubt if Wilkos, who is a big guy and a former cop, said that to her. That is what she said to *him* and he did what all men do: listened and then nodded his head in sheepish agreement. These same women, of course, offer no guarantees that they will, in turn, keep their hands to themselves. The sister-dyke will take full advantage of and in such a "relationship."

"Jerry Springer" is a show that should be banned, not because of what takes place on the stage when people fight about everything from infidelity and adultery to stealing money, but what could potentially happen when these people leave the studio and return home. On these programs the men stand as the culprits and the women complain. If a woman messes over a man, all he can do is stand there crying and whining and, even if vindicated, he moves on without incident. Women on this show are allowed, not only to fight one another (pull hair, rip off wigs, tear of blouses, wrestle to the floor and expose their panties), but more importantly to this particular essay, they get to slap the living shit out of the man.

One show featured a young dude who went to California to do porn, got talked into gay porn and had to tell his girl on stage. It was all about the money he claims. When he told her on the stage of "Springer," she looked at him and said, "If we weren't on TV right now, I'd smack you." This means she's smacked him before when they weren't on television, and he didn't hit her back. This is a guy who is athletically built, and she's some little short white woman. So the question is, where is the motivation, where is the inspiration to make these women KNOW that they can strike a man, apparently whenever they want to, and not have to worry about being retaliated against? Such a woman, with such an attitude and history, though white, clearly has the characteristics of the "sister-dyke."

Maury Povich, following Springer's lead, adds a different twist: he uses lie detector tests to find out if either party is being truthful or is telling a lie when it comes to the paternity of children. This program has, on a number of occasions, allowed a woman to slap the living shit out of a man or to threaten to do so.

The movie, "Haywire" featured a skilled woman beating the living shit out of man after man and, even when they attacked her or instigated the confrontation, it is clear that she was not only going to defeat them but humiliate her adversary as well. The CW Channel has a show, "Arrow," which is about some wannabe super hero who carries a bow and arrow and fights evil. Lately he's come across a female counterpart (wouldn't you know it) who unmercifully beats the shit out of men. If you get a chance to view it, juxtapose the two "heroes" and their fighting styles: the man head hunts and breaks jaws combined with a few kicks, but this female goes straight for the testicles and lower body shots. What's that about?

It is popular culture, spurred by magazines, television, and the social network, that is perpetuating this, ""that's okay to be a dyke" bullshit. Young girls in middle school think it's cute to kiss each other and "experiment" with girl-girl dating. Women enrolling in what we called "self-defense" classes, but really they're classes that train them to focus on men's nuts. You can use your knees, you can kick or you can duck and land a jab – as long as you it him in the nuts, he'll be disabled.

Finally, as long as men keep fucking up – and we will -- the sister-dyke ranks will grow and inevitably become more visible. Black men are abandoning their families, chasing white women, hanging out in bars, getting fucked up on alcohol and drugs, taking it up the ass from their "pals," and a host of other things that the police and media protect white men from being caught doing. So if we know that, all we gotta do is to stop fucking up. The sister-dyke might be a genetic reality, born a lesbian. But whether the tendencies come from nature or from nurture, she's here to stay. Some will try to disguise it, some will be outright including public displays of affection.

Facts are facts: roles have changed because of personal, social and cultural need, and the recent approval of homosexual marriage. The sister-dyke, as quiet as it's kept, is the protector of our community and in some cases, of our secrets. You normally don't see her on TV babbling about her Black family concerns like these bitch-like male assholes are prone to do.

CHAPTER 2:

Black Man as Childlike/ Quasi-Feminine "Metro Male"

The black man has revisited his role as societal "coon." And this time, it's by choice. During the initial phase the role was imposed on him and he was paraded out for people to laugh at. In the modern version, Today the black man seems to relish his gayness to the point where he seeks it out and then, once off camera or off stage, he extends this role as everybody's "joke" into real life.

On a segment of "The Real Husbands of Beverly Hills," George Takei (Sulu of Star Trek) is at a fundraiser with Nick Cannon and tells the audience, "Gay is the new Black." Well, my theory is a little different: when it comes to Black men, Black is the new gay. Let me explain.

Let's name some of these new black metro males: Michael Strayhan, Stephen A. Smith, Michael Steele, P. Diddy, Russell Westbrook, Kanye West, Tyler Perry, Anthony Anderson, Nelly, Cam Newton, Will Smith, Chris Bosh, Taye Diggs, Russell Simmons and Colin Kaepernick, to name but a few.

And don't talk to me about, "but he's married," or "he's got kids" or "he's got a girlfriend." To this black metro male, don't none of that mean a damn thing. In fact there is a huge supply of women who are more than willing to marry gay black men (if they have money) and men on the downlow. And these women will protect the identities of these guys in exchange for access to their finances. It seems to be a growing trend.

This shit ain't on purpose. The black man is the new homosexual: emasculated, quasi- feminine and as a result, non-threatening. Then there's Ray Rice a 27-year old pro football player, a running back who was placed on indefinite suspension because he was caught on a videotape, in an elevator, knocking his wife out. He then dragged her out of an elevator and now he's lost his job. All that money is gone. But that's not what pisses me off. If you watch the video, this woman (a sister-dyke) is walking all up on rice pointing her finger at him - the way you would do to someone whose ass you felt you could kick. Evidently, she was wrong.

You might say that he wasn't acting like a homosexual – he was a "macho man" and he hit her. No, you're looking at it ass backwards. Before he hit her she was walking up on him, castigating him, pointing her finger as if she had done this before. She had no fear of him based on what she had said and done before. He had his cell phone in one hand, but look at her actions toward him. Was she afraid? No. Her actions constitute an assault by law. He blazed on her and knocked her out

– but she started it. She had no fear – *she was treating this man as if he was another bitch!*

Her actions are what takes place when you have a society talking about "never hit a woman." If a woman knows you won't hit her, she will assault YOU! Look at that elevator videotape: this is a woman that believes that she can do whatever she wants, and she's walking up on a professional football player. He defended himself and now he's a laughing stock. Then he thought that marrying her would change things. It didn't, but now she's got him in another bind -- only this one is legally sanctioned. Can you say "take me to the cleaners"?

But she had no respect for his size because she didn't see an athlete – she saw a faggot. Here's what I say: If somebody violates your personal space, you have a right to get them off you, I don't care what gender they are. After all, we're supposed to be "equal," remember?

America's new childlike quasi-gay entity is *none other than the African-American male.* Tupac Shakur referred to them as "bitch ass niggas." He doesn't mean that they were gay, but that they were cowards and weak. You can see how the once "supermasculine menial" has become, over the years, nothing more than an effeminate has-been, diamond earring-wearing, freakishly pitiful joke. He's what the kids in the street would refer to as "a pussy." The black man is a shadow and antithesis of his former 1960s "say it loud, I'm black and I'm proud" self. In simpler terms, the black man of the 21st century is an effeminate and womanish shadow of his former self.

Michele Wallace correctly outlines the rhetoric of the 1960s "black power" movement, which was slowly turned into a kind of socio-psychological rationale or justification for the devalued role of the Black woman in the Movement:

> The picture drawn for us over and over again is of a man
> who is a child, who is the constant victim of unholy
> alliance between his woman and the enemy, the white man.
> It is an emotional interpretation but it has also been used by
> the contemporary black man to justify his oppression of the
> black woman, to justify his getting ahead by walking over
> her prostrate body. "I don't owe you anything, black woman
> because (1) you sold me out and (2) you've always been
> ahead anyway." The facts are a good deal more
> complicated and ambiguous. (Wallace, 1978: 18-19)

See? And the reason her words weren't more widely distributed is because she (Michele Wallace) is a dyke herself! But the truth is the truth no matter who speaks it.

What do you read about in today's papers when a black child has been abused or killed or a black person has been shot by a cop? The black man, who would have at one time burned something down or dealt with the system in some other confrontative way, expresses "outrage." His collective power is viewed by those in power as nothing more than an "outcry." Like a scatter-brained old bitch who got her purse snatched, the black man of today cries, whimpers, begs, prays, wishes, hopes and does everything else but confront the system. The system, being as evil as it is and being run by the self-proclaimed demi-gods that I wrote about elsewhere, views such cowardice as compliance and agreement, and simply continues to heap hell upon the heads of the black man in particular and the black family (what's left of it) as a whole.

Dr. Frances Cress Welsing alluded to this over three decades ago when she talked about how the black man is being punked. She described how he refers to his home as a "crib" and allows the woman to call him "baby." In addition to that, Welsing says that the role of "man" has been taken up by someone else (I say it's the white woman) and this leaves him nothing more than the role of "boy." Sitting around playing video games all day - not young kids but grown ass men -- and then bragging about it.

As a matter of fact, during an April 19, 2015 segment of "Judge Mathis," the plaintiff and defendant were arguing about a man and whose boyfriend he was. The plaintiff said, "we talked about if she was with him or not and she said, "naw, he's just a baby." She explained, "That's what we call men, babies." Say what? During an episode of "Married With Children," Peg told her neighbor Marcy that, "men are basically children with paychecks."

Grown men playing video games under conditions as bad as these? The old song used to say, "Here's our chance to dance our way out of our constrictions." And that's just what we're doing; like Nero, we're fiddling while Rome (the communities we live in) burns. And the persnickety black man, still feared because of his skin color and dick length, is really a fag she black clothing.

And then there's the "feminization" factor. Sitting in beauty parlors with rollers in his hair, wearing earrings and diamond bracelets, wearing gold plates over his real teeth. Just the fact that he's obsessed with being well-groomed over being well-informed speaks volumes right there. And those fuckin' earrings, which these punks think are the "in" thing, are just indicators that this nigga has some money and don't know what to do with it. So he becomes a bitch, inclusive of skinny jeans, flip-flops and hair gel.

As evidence, during a September 7, 2015 edition of "The First 48," the Dallas cops have this young guy in the interrogation room and they ask him to identify one of his homies, Justin Jones, taken from a public camera. He does and then they ask him, "what is this he has on his head?" You know what it was? The snitch says, "That's his girl friend's sleeping cap. She wears it every day." In other words, this wanna be thug, who had just killed a white dude in cold blood and then jacked a car, is walking around like a bitch with a sleeping cap on his head. The cops go the the woman's house. When they arrested her, she had on a sleeping cap! "It was an incident where me and Kushy was together … I didn't even know Kushy had a gun," she said in the interrogation room.

Curlers. Sleeping caps. Earrings. Skinny jeans. These young dudes are more bitch-like than any previous generation, including those that wore conks and platform shoes!

I see these professional athletes – Deon Sanders, Ray Lewis, LeBron James, Dez Bryant, Dewyane Wade, Barry Bonds, and many others -- wearing diamond earrings. Do those black muthafuckas know how much African slave-type work went into mining those diamonds? The Jews who buy those diamonds from those mining companies sure know. But like the Black man's sexual behavior, the information is kept on the "downlow."

And furthermore, what's the point: are they psychological bitches, that is, do they want to be women or what? So what if it's "the style"? This is some feminine gay-type shit if you ask me. When added to what I've already described, can you not see that there has been a "transformation" and that black men are the new gays? The only "threat" we represent is in the white man's mind when he sees one of our kids walking toward him on the street. Other than that, we are a bunch of down-low, happy-to-have-a-job sissies!

Back in the day when I was coming up, we'd refer to someone adorning themselves this say as "punks" or "sissies." But we had our weird styles too: platform shoes (basically high heels), skin tight slacks (basically skinny jeans), silk shirts open at the collar (basically blouses) and so on. Huge rings on damn hear every finger and those infernal medallions that we wore around our necks. Trying to be cute and, in fact, many black men who think they look good refer to themselves as "pretty" or as "pretty boys."

This brings us to another issue, the rise of homosexual behavior or outright "gay discovery" in America, and in particular, the "downlow behavior" or black men and the claim that there is such a thing as "bisexuality."

To begin with, let us dismiss this shit about "bisexuality." How can you be bisexual unless you have a dick AND a vagina? In terms of behavior, how can you be bisexual: either you like pussy or you like balls banging across your forehead! It's either one or the other. You've got young girls and boys in middle- and high school going around talking about being "bisexual" because that's what they hear older kids and adults saying. How absurd! If you're in prison and you get raped or rape another prisoner, does that mean you're bisexual? No, but guess what: in my book if you're fucking other guys in the ass, or giving them head, you're gay!

This brings up another subject: the downlow - men have sex with other men even though they may have wives or girlfriends at home.

<u>The Downlow and the Black "Metro Male"</u>

Cities like Omaha and Dallas are full of these freaks. The more on the downlow they are, the more macho they try to act, the more boisterous their voices and the more "black than thou" the organization they are a part of. And the more likely they are to get jobs and keep those jobs from the homoerotic white man. For instance, a group called "100 Black Men." Why? There's not even a hundred of them. It's a smokescreen, and with the headquarters being in Washington, DC – home of the downlow – then it's got to be a dupe. There is at least one fraternity I know of, the one that barks and acts like they're so crazy about women, that is KNOWN for screwing young girls and also has leadership that is on the downlow.

Morehouse College, an all-black school in another fag hotspot, Atlanta, is also the home of the college fag. Fag groups on campus have cliques and they are not shy about it. But in my book any fraternity (all men) is a prelude for homosexual behavior and in some of them (I've heard) such behavior is part of the initiation test.

Super-tom and "coon" Michael Strahan, a former member of the New York Giants vaunted defense, is now the new "likeable nigger" that the white man has programmed. His gimmick is this huge gap in his teeth, but you know he's got his "punk-ass pedigree" if you just look at his track record.

First, Strahan was married to a white woman. They have twin girls and the kids are black, and he's recently appeared in a commercial with them. He also boasts about and has them on his morning show, which is called, "Live with Kelly and Michael." . Now this blonde white girl, Kelly Ripa, got away with marrying Mark Consuelos , a Latino brother and he's pumped her full of brown babies. But now she's hosting a morning show, prime time, with this giant black man. But never fear – he's as coonish as they come and the white man knows it. They hold hands, hug each other, and appear "so nice together" to a white morning public, mostly females.

But before that, Strahan was married to a white woman, but they had a bitter divorce and what was the first thing she charged him with? Being a fag! That's right. The news articles including the *New York Daily News*, carried a story that Jean Strahan accused her husband of having an extramarital affair with another man, TV doctor Ian Smith. According to the news reports, Strahan (Mike) moved into Ian's one bedroom apartment "and you can say an alternative lifestyle sprouted." The report said that her lawyer then stopped her before she could elaborate, and the attorney, who was speaking for Mike, denied a sexual relationship between Smith and Strahan.

`Now, check this out: Strahan went on the Wendy Williams radio show and dismissed the allegations. "If this were true, it would hit the fan from the get go," he said. "I have plenty of friends that are bi- or homosexual. It's fine with me. This is New York City. If you can't accept people for being people, then you have no business being here." What??? But it gets worse: "I don't frown on anybody for that lifestyle, it's not my lifestyle. And you know, I just laugh. All that matters is that I'm gonna take care of my kids."

Maybe he had a case and the white women was out for blood. But the fact that he is an Uncle Tom is without a doubt. Why else would decision makers put him on the air, during prime time, with this boney little white girl? Just watch him during his appearances on FOX NFL Football on Sundays. He's playing around with Jimmy Johnson, Howie Long and Terry Bradshaw, cracking jokes like a scatter-brained old bitch. And then, during the trial of several years ago, here is how this bullet-headed muthafucka explained the homo allegations: "As for staying with Smith, Strahan said: "When I had to stay somewhere, he opened his door. It's not that I couldn't stay at any hotel I want."

Bingo! Strahan is a multi-millionaire in the middle of a divorce. He could have gotten a suite at any of those nice hotels in New York and recruited all kinds of women. Instead, he chose to stay in a one-bedroom apartment with a MAN. What is that shit about? The downlow, I tell ya. Smith's explanation was as weak as Strahan's. Smith said that, because he is a "happily married man," it was impossible for him to have been in a sexual relationship with Strahan.

Impossible? Nigga please! If he's so happily married and he's a doctor, why in the hell is he living on a one-bedroom apartment? I don't really give a shit about how homosexuals live their lives, but I do have a concern and that is this: why are these downlow niggas lying about it? And furthermore why do they think they're NOT gay when they engage in it. You just had your dick in another man's ass or you had his dick in your mouth. How does that NOT make you gay? Black men, from super macho to what we've been reduced to: what Karenga once referred to as nothing more than "a set of reactions to white people" (Karenga, 1967). And it was also Karenga, with all his flaws, who nevertheless hit the nail on the proverbial head when he wrote, "The negro was made and manufactured in America." I would add so is the new fag -- the African-American male.

And that's the point here, isn't it? *The black man is a man in name only.* He's working for somebody, serving somebody, kowtowing to somebody and so on. He's lifeless unless there is someone around to give his life meaning and magnitude, form or function. His woman sees this shit and the days of pitying him and charging it to his being "an endangered species," she now treats him (and deservedly so) like "endangered feces."

From on-going references to "the wife," "my old lady," "the old ball and chain," or "my bitch," to "moms," "mother dear," "big mama" and so on, *the black man of today is a punk waiting for orders or searching for someone to give him some orders.*

A commercial for Swiffers mops has a huge black man (the family surname is the Bells) at home with his kid. "I'm Jerry Bell the first," and the kid says, "I'm Jerry Bell the second." He adds, "I'm like a big bear and he's my little cub." Now, the committee that reviewed this commercial while and after it was made, obviously thought this shit was cute. But why should a black man, somewhat burly at that, have to "beastify" himself for a commercial that has to do with a cleaning product? Is he a fuckin' bear? No. Do white people think that big black menare animals? Yes. So racism is justified as long as the white version of reality is appeased.

Obviously married to a white woman, this kid comes in and out of the house tracking up the floor with mud. This stupid muthafucka who is supposed to be his father, instead of telling the kid to stop fucking up, simply gets up each time and mops up behind the kid. So fucked up is he that somebody leaves a case of Swiffers on his front step. Now he has the "Swiffer Wet Jet" mop and the pads that come associated with it. Now he can happily mop ups and talks about how much "fun" it is. In fact, at one point in the commercial to show what a house broken punk he is, he actually says, "It's kinda fun." Like a slave that's been programmed to accept toil and menial work, this oversized asshole has learned to "suffer peacefully."

At the end of the commercial he flops back down on "deep couch city" with his half-white kid and the two relax.

Let me tell you what the problem is. First of all, he admits that mopping that floor "all the time," behind the mud that his bad ass kid is tracking in, makes his back hurt. Instead of teaching that kid the error of his ways, it is implied that he just sits there and waits for the kid – and his kids friends according to him – to keep tracking mud into the house. Each time he "has" to get up and mop it. Somebody leaves a case of Swiffer pads for his mop and he's in seventh heaven; still mopping, still waiting for his kid to fuck shit up. His bitch is obviously at the job, so he's the "house husband." The problem, in my view, is the kid still doesn't respect the floor or his father and the black guy has adapted his role as the household bitch.

A commercial by AFLAC makes a presentation that includes both the white woman as the new white male and the black male as the new metro male or "faggot." This commercial mainly appears during football games, college and pro, and I've seen it most often on ESPN.

The scene is a weight room and the white woman is pushing major iron. Each time the AFLAC duck interrupts her but in her assertive role, it's no big deal. She has on short sweats, pussy lips visible and a bra that, when she bends over for the weight, exposes her miniature breasts. The black man is lifting weights and when he reaches for them, the duck appears quacking and he sheepishly backs off on his hands and feet in a reverse position. The scene then switches to the two of them together and he tells the woman about the AFLAC insurance benefits. But he still shows fear and, sure enough, at the end of the commercial as he reaches for a towel, he accidentally grabs the duck's ass, the duck quacks and the black "man" sheepishly backs off like a true faggot.

Here is how a website called Ispot.TV.com describes it:

> In this commercial that aired during NBC's hit show "The Voice" and ABC's "The Muppets," the Aflac Duck is a gym duck. He sneezes "Aflac!!" when his gym mate claps powdery dust in his face. Then, he does what looks like snow angel movements on the ground while the woman lifts heavy weights, and he pops up from out of nowhere when a man tries to lift a huge tire. Oh, and the man later reaches into the pile of towels and accidentally grabs the Aflac Duck by the tail. As the duck soon relaxes on a ball, the man shares with the woman how the duck helped him out with One Day Pay. Now that is one serious duck.

To white folks, it's probably perfectly innocent. But remember: there are committees and teams of people who review these commercials before they hit the air. The sponsors have to approve them. And that is for a reason: the black man is totally harmless and the white woman is the more aggressive of the two. The woman sees the duck as harmless while in both instances, the "black man" shows fear and confusion.

A commercial by Fingerhut.com shows two black men in what could be viewed as a somewhat compromising position. One black man is in a double bed lying down surfing on his smart phone. There is a pillow next to him but nobody else is in the bed. In walks this fat guy with a t-shirt on and a hat. He starts leaning over the back of this other guy and they're conversing. And guess what they're talking about? Shopping! Like two bitches! The fat one knows almost everything there is to know about the discounts and the merchandise that Fingerhut allegedly has to offer. The guy in the bed just so happens to have a laptop in bed with him as he scans the information being offered by the fat dude.

In the next scene the fat guy flops down on a lounging chair that happens to be in the room and falls fast asleep. What's this shit about? What does it imply? What committee came up with this idea and who approved it? In simpler terms, where's the bitches?! And furthermore, are these two assholes a couple or are they just on the "downlow"?

Allstate Insurance airs a commercial that is both dyke-like and metro- male-ish. She asks him, "So you say men are superior drivers?" And then she flashes a check she gets for having a flawless driving record for six months. The man sitting there is stuttering, acting like a scatter-brained old bitch, and every time he gets ready to say something she cuts him off, with the voice that she is using being that of spokesman Dennis Hasbert, this black man who has a deep monotone sound ("The Unit," "Heat," "Navy Seals"). In other words, she's a woman when it comes to getting the check, but in order to put her man in his place, she has to revert to a male persona. The message is that men ain't shit and a woman is superior but when it comes down to brass tacks, she can "use" the voice of a man whenever she chooses. This time it's the voice of a black man.

Lowes Home Improvement has a commercial that shows the gradual "faggotization" of the black male. A black man is watering his lawn and white white neighbor compliments him on it. The black man says, "Yeah they told me what to do and it really looks good. You know I'm beginning to feel like I can do anything." And what is this fags concept of "doing anything." He tells his neighbor he wants to learn how to "fold fitted sheets." How much more bitch-like can you get? Then the commercial cuts to him in the bedroom, next to the bed, struggling with a fitted sheet. He finally throws it to the ground and stomps on it.

In another commercial (aired on FX), this one for ___, this black guy is sitting in his living room and the dog tracks mud across a white shag throw rug. This asshole sends off for the product and cleans the rug. His young daughter then does the same thing as she walks in the opposite direction, tracking mud across the same throw rug, totally disrespecting him. This quasi-fag does nothing but sit there, rolls his eyes like a bitch, thereby accepting his role as someone who relies on this product to deal with a dog that should be getting his ass kicked and a young daughter who should be corrected and chastised.

In an Old Spice commercial being aired in September of 2015, muscular Terry Crews ("The Expendables") is shown promoting the product. At one point he turns into a woodpecker (bird's body, his head) and pecks into a tree. The commercial then morphs into a house scene where the muscular black guy who won awards for promoting Old Spice back in the day (gay?) is sitting at a table with no shirt on, looking like a true fag. In another Old Spice commercial, aired in December of 2015, Crews and the same guy are shown as buddies. Crews has on some tight gym shorts and the other black man only has on a towel. At one point they are together on a double-seater bicycle. They even grow old together, and they have a scrapbook that is titled "Friendship." The tag line has something to do with "Smellmitment." What?

This is the kind of "metro male" imagery that America has clearly accepted: the image-oriented promotion of what Eldridge Cleaver once referred to as, "the supermasculine menial."

AT&T has a couple of insulting commercials that were aired during September of 2015. One rips off Gil Scott Heron's great statement that, "the revolution will not be televised" and claims, "The revolution WILL be televised – and mobilized." This insult will fly right over the heads of the millennials. The second one features a young brutha (the one who played the young kid in the old movie, "Fresh") who is working for AT&T at the counter and tells a client, "we can solve all problems." They then discuss some issues with the young black man adding, "I like to bake." Is this guy a fag or what?

Another commercial, this one for Mountain Dew's drink, Kickstart, provides a subtle example of the physically in shape black man and his sissified tendencies. This commercial is also a prime example of the downlow at work.

The commercial shows NBA star (Oklahoma Thunder) Russell Westbrook and three other dudes getting ready to "go out." Russell enters the room and declares, "Wazzup fellas! Let's get the night started." (not "party," but "night"). And the clock behind him reads 8:15. So what are they going to do until it's time to hit the clubs? That's usually about 11:00. That means three hours - four guys -and whatever they're about to do before the high-energy Kickstart wears off, they better do it quick. Hmmmm what could it be? "Time to get started" Westbrook declares. (To do *what,* I wonder?)

Russell orders, "Let's go!" and the foursome is off. They only get as far as the top of the stairs in the foyer. Headed to get involved in some downlow behavior, perhaps? As they sip the drink at the top of the stairs, Westbrook judges how each of his "pals" look: all clad in tight fitting shirts and skinny jeans - truly a group of down low niggas which basically means fags.

Russell has guzzled his drink, and is magically transformed, now dressed in a white shirt. As they prance to the foyer of the house, the second guy sips, and he receives a silver/gray shirt to which Westbrook exclaims, "That's a dope shirt!" The other two guys, shorter than Westbrook and the other guy (or perhaps standing on a lower rung of the stairs) upon observing Westbrook's approval, hastily sip their drinks. But when the magic shirt appears for those two, they are both inside of the same shirt like some Siamese twins (read: faggots). Russell sees it and says, "That's messed up."

Just like a group of bitches getting ready to go clubbin', these downlow niggas take a sip of an energy soda and get ready to head somewhere to take care of business. But in my view, the entire commercial is homerotic.

Russell Westbrook and his "fashion style," is clearly that of a sissy. In a website promo it is written that, Oklahoma City Thunder point guard Russell Westbrook is one of the most unique dressers in the NBA off the court, so naturally, he has teamed up with Barneys New York to release a new clothing line to add some flair to your on-court look. Westbrook's line, which works in cooperation with Jordan Brand, features elephant-print Dri-FIT athletic shirts and matching basketball shorts, along with a few other accessories you can wear on or off the court.

"In a television commercial for his brand, The Russell Westbrook XO Barneys New York collection, he's walking down the street as the camera, shooting from below, shows him in white tight jeans and deck sneakers. He keeps walking and then he's shown with his shirt totally off. What does that have to do with what he's selling - that is, unless he's selling his ASS?! As evidence, witness his new see through shirts, exposing nipples (a point made by "His and Hers" co-host Jamelle Hill) that was discussed on the September 15, 2015 segment of that show. Is this dude a fag or what?

On August 26, 2015 it was reported and shown on someone's video that Westbrook was at a Taylor Swift concert singing the tune "We Are Never Ever Ever Getting Back Together" by Taylor Swift. What kind of effeminate bullshit is this? During an August 27, 2105 segment of "First Take" Stephen A. Smith (effeminate himself) referred to Westbrook's behavior as "eccentric." No, it's more than that: Westbrook even acts feminine when he's not on the court, and his ultra-aggressive style on the court might be attributed to a "hate all men" attitude that more than a few bitches seem to have in this day and age.

In September of 2015 Westbrook did a commercial for US Cellular and looked more like a faggot than ever before. The commercial begins with the narrator telling us that, "There's a million sides to basketball star and fashion icon Russell Westbrook." (I'll say!) At any rate, Westbrook dons a number of costumes reflecting the roles of different people who could get good reception no matter where they were. He was a farmer in skin tight overalls in the middle of a field selling "Russell's Brussels" , he was a paleontologist, he was a park ranger in a tight uniform and several other roles. The slogan is, "you can do all the things you like." I've got a strange feeling that Westbrook likes the same thing that gay men like. As for the commercial, it was well-acted, but it is clear that there is something effeminate about this hard-playing NBA all-star. There may be something psychological that is a little "off" as well.

At about the same time Direct TV began airing these commercials that even further "faggotized" a black athlete. Randy Moss, one of the greatest wide receivers in NFL history, is better known as being his own man and doing what he wants to do. He was labeled a "black sheep" and shunned because he wouldn't give up smoking weed. Now he's a broadcaster and has been "broken in" by the white man, and he must have passed whatever "let us dick you in the ass" tests they gave him, because this Direct TV commercial is truly an insult to this young brutha.

In the commercial there are two Randy Moss characters. One is the 6'4" brutha in a suit who subscribes to Direct TV. The other one introduced himself as "petite Randy Moss," and he's about 5'4". First of all, why "petite" Randy Moss? Why not "tiny Randy Moss," "reduced size Randy Moss," "miniature Randy Moss" or something of that type? A group full of advertising experts sat in a room and came up with "petite" because being petite does not just mean small, but also implies being "feminine."

So we have the petite Randy Moss, dressed like a sissy and in the next scene, he's in an aisle of a grocery store jumping up and down because he's too short to reach up high where the "fruitie munch" cereal is located. Why this name for the serial? I'll tell you why: because "fruitie" is a slang word for homosexual, that's why. And Moss signed on to this shit in exchange for money, and put this image out there, one that will be immortalized in the white man's history banks. Like Westbrook, if he pisses off whitey, he will forever be dubbed a "fag." Randy wasn't the only athlete that has been "bitchified."

In December of 2015 Cam Newton did a commercial for ___. He walks into the workout room and is preparing to use the whirlpool bath to soak. In the bath is a white boy. Cam tells him, "You know you're in my lucky tank, right?" The white boy, who has on ear phones, simply waves him him off. Cam also has his ear phones but tells the other guy, "Alright you bought this on yourself." He then proceeds to climb into the small soaking tub with this white man. Is this homoerotic behavior or what?

And some of the imagery is not so overt, as we can see in a commercial for the new Nissan Sentra. A black woman picks up a black man on the way to the game in her new Nissan Sentra. As they head to the stadium (Nissan Stadium in Tennessee obviously on the way to a Titans football game), they engage in conversation about the game and the team. She tells him, "Our linebackers and DBs (Defensive Backs) dish it out," and You'll see," and he adds, "I think my boys have a shot this year." Not to let him get in the last word, she adds, "especially with this new offense." As she spreads on her eye black beneath her eyes as if she's going to be playing, still driving, she says, "Our running back is a beast, and once he hits the hole, he's gone…"

In simpler terms, she's playing the role of the knowledgeable fan (read: male) and he's acting like a bitch. To add insult to injury, as they get out of the car and walk toward the stadium, she pats him on his effeminate ass. (aired in November of 2015). A clear-cut case of role reversal.

In the following sub-areas of "politics" and "popular culture," I will elaborate further on society's "new gay" (some might say "new fag"), the African American male. Read it and weep.

Politics

Hanes Walton Jr. once wrote a book called *Black Politics* and, during the time the book was being used in Black Studies Departments all over the nation, it served as an excellent primer and overview of black political power in the traditional American realm, touched briefly on black nationalism, and was a relevant text for its time and context.

But looking back at the black existence in this country, can there really be such a thing as "black politics," or are were merely looking at white politics in blackface? Can a black city councilman, a black county supervisor, or a black mayor really have political power when they sit on boards where they are outnumbered and when most of the issues they deal with are about empowering the city they live in? Does the black presence in these positions really make a difference? Even at the mayor position, can a black mayor really do anything more than work toward making the white municipality and all its institutions, better?

Are there any black mayors of note? Most have been set up by the white power structure to fail and many have been nothing more than thieves who live nowhere near the black community. The few I can remember - Coleman Young, Harold Washington, Marion Barry, Kwame Kilpatrick, and a few more - were either killed in office (Harold Washington) or disgraced and cut loose. In their place are the effeminate, soft, "metro-male" who becomes a leader because he tows the line. He is the new faggot, under the guise of "metro-male."

Politics is defined by some as "the art and science of using power." Black men in this country don't have any "power." Karenga (1994) charged that black politicians don't have power but are, for the most part, "influence peddlers." Some might have some visibility (especially at the local levels) and out of that might come some influence. But that's about it. The real black men who use to exist in the 1960s and 1960s went for the jugular when they confronted the white man. Today's black metro-males are so gutless that their version of working in the community means finding interested white people, hooking up with them, and then paving the way for white invasions of the community.

Today's metro-male black man will gladly sell out the masses for a place at the white man's table. Like Malcolm X said about the "house negro," today's leader kowtows to whatever their white "masters" need and demand. That's the way it is in Omaha, in Milwaukee, and Dallas. I am in the process of researching other cities.

In my view, religion should be placed under the heading of politics, especially the way it is performed and practiced here in America. One of my Master's degrees is in political science, so I have studied this nation's political structures and its documents, especially the Constitution. I am well aware of how these white men viewed their religious beliefs and how those were imposed upon their people, the Native Americans (the ones that they didn't kill off), and later on, upon the African people they kidnapped and bought to the southern shores of this country. So while many believe that politics is moral I am of the belief that morality is political.

The ministers, deacons, bishops and others who lead the African-American church may be married, but far too many of them are not only womanizers, but also on the downlow. Like Catholic priests, these Baptist leaders are screwing little boys, under-age girls and female members of the church, who are husband-hunting and hot as hell. Many may be sister-dykes fronting in a search for a man (read: additional paycheck), but if they want another woman, there are plenty to be found in the pews of the Black church.

Most of the ministers oppose being gay – but gays have money so these ministers are more than happy to make exceptions. But the fact of the matter is that many of these loud talking hallelujah hucksters are as feminine as any man can get. And guess what? The congregation knows who they are, what they are doing and yet forgives them almost every single time.

<u>Popular Culture</u>

Even though Priest of the movie "SuperFly" made the long hair (known then as the Jesus Christ hairstyle) something that black women and men admired, he was no punk - he stood for something. Sure, he sold drugs, but he also fought, and defeated, his oppressor and them left America and helped work to save Africa in the sequel, "SuperFly TNT." But today on the screen all you see are comedians, flunkies and punks.

In an August 2014 commercial for Tide detergent, having informed the viewing audience that they are a married couple with a family of five (obviously through blending), a wimpish-looking black man and a black woman are sitting on the couch folding clothes fresh out of the dryer. As the commercial ends she pulls up a pair of blue shorts/underwear that appear to be for a child. She thinks the draws belong to their young daughter, but the black man, her husband, reaches over and says, "those are mine." When she expresses shock, and asks, "Seriously?" he says, "No they aren't." Then, when she settles down he admits, "Yes they are." She looks at the screen and says, "Okay…." as if to imply, "this is one weird muthafucka I'm married to." Say what?

More than that, she sleeps with this brutha. Shouldn't she be able to distinguish between her young daughters multi-colored panties and this niggas "tighties"? What's going on there and who approved this kind of bullshit? White folks are going to see it and wonder if this is the kind of shit that is going on behind closed doors with "those negroes." More importantly, what type of image does this commercial send to the women and children sitting in front of the television and who are long-time Tide detergent customers?

In October of 2014, yet another commercial for some type of cell phones has a brother sneaking around with a cell phone while his family shops in the mall. He hides behind a beam in the mall, but backs right into his wife. When she asks him if he's watching the game, he tells her "no," that he's recording her favorite movie. Once again, the wimpy black man has to "explain" to his wife (read: mother figure). He chooses to lie as he changes the screen on the phone. The woman rolls her eyes at him as if to say, "lying motherfucker" and the little girl, who walked up with the mother rolls her beautiful big eyes at him too, as if to say, "nigga, your game is weak." Then they take hands and walk out of the mall as a threesome, with the little girl in the middle.

During August and September of 2014, in a commercial for Go-Gurt yogurt, the father and son are in the kitchen preparing the son's lunch. The son is watching as the father is placing an extra yogurt in the child's lunch pail. "Mom doesn't let me have extra," he says. The father says, "Well mom's not here so today we do it dad's way…" says the father, and the child adds, "which means I get TWO." Then in unison, they chant, " "snack time and lunch/snack time and lunch" as they begin dancing, doing "the robot" as the scene winds to an end.

So only when the woman is gone can these two males – one a boy and one a man – do as they please or do what is right. In my view, this makes BOTH of them "boys." In other words, when mama's gone, he can pretend to be a REAL man and make a decision, but he's teaching his son that mama is the boss, as in "when the cat's gone, the mice will play."

On October 2, 2014, NBC aired the Green Bay Packers vs. Minnesota Vikings game as part of its weekly "Thursday Night Football" fare. In describing rookie black quarterback Teddy Bridgewater who was not playing because of an injury, they talked about his talent but added how "humble" he was. During the October 12, 2014 game with Minnesota playing the Detroit Lions, one of the commentators again described Bridgewater as, "cerebral, good work ethic, and extremely humble." Also during that October 2 competition, co-commentator Phil Simms made a comment about African-American announcer James Brown who was standing on the sidelines. They talked about his nice suit and the fact that "he always has a nice smile."

What kind of shit is this? Why don't these white boys just come out and dub these black men as "good niggers"? These kinds of comments and descriptions hails back to the 1950s when white folks felt like "being a good nigger" or "acting white" were compliments. But that is what the black man has come to: an effeminate lump of skin and blood who apparently only seeks to "serve," kiss ass, smile, dance and "look cute."

In a commercial for Cox Cable, a black woman is standing up on an upside laundry basket pledging her commitment to Cox and its technology. She then says that she can watch whatever she wants and insulting the "science fiction nonsense" that her husband is watching in the next room. He childishly quips that he doesn't care what she says because he's "in a parallel universe."

But look closely: while she's pontificating all over the living room in front of two young children, he's in another room, on a lap top – on a single bed. This bitch-ass nigga (the man) says, "I don't even hear you. I'm in a parallel universe." This nigga is so beaten down that he escapes into fantasy and forgets all about the fact that two kids are in the living room. So she's the boss and the single bed suggests that they don't even sleep together.

In a 2015 commercial for Metro PCS cell phones, a young black couple is sitting in a lobby waiting on someone to service them. She asks him, "who taught you about Mero PCS?" and he answers, "you did, sweetie." Then she asks, "And who taught you about common sense?" He's embarrassed so he covers his mouth and coughs out the answer, "you did." Say what? Come to think of it, maybe if he had common sense he wouldn't be with a bitch who would ask that insulting question. And at the same time, she's a stupid bitch for being with someone who she had to teach about common sense.

In 2014 Dunking Donuts was running a commercial that had to be screened by entire committees before it was approved for national syndication – as are all commercials. The screeners have to make sure that the commercial touches upon all the salient points, doesn't offend any group, and that it's "catchy." This commercial is one more example of the wimpish, "I'm sorry mom" attitude that the black man has adopted when it comes to women. And apparently, the sheepish shit-eating is not viewed as offensive by advertisers or viewers.

The black man is waiting in the car and the black woman gets in. She asks him if he's been eating smoked sausage. Instead of this muthafucka telling her that he did (although it's none of her fuckin' business) he says "no." It's a Dunkin

Donuts sausage and he wolfed it down so she couldn't get any – the way a child would do. Totally emasculated, as well as being a coward and a liar.

How about these "nigga flicks" that Tyler Perry is producing? Unrealistic to a fault, his movies imply that black people are just as insane as whites when it comes to their personal relationships. Here we have a gay male (Perry) who refuses to admit it and wants everyone to believe that he's heterosexual. Today's black "metro male" acts like more of a bitch than women do. You can hear it in his ideas and statements regarding history and this system, you can see it in his choice of clothing, his absence from the family system, and is apparent liking for literally and figuratively taking it up the ass from the system and, of course other males.

When it comes to television and film, we've all seen the black police captain with no power, the man who subordinates laugh at and ridicule every chance they get. A man who has been rendered impotent. Recall Captain Dobey on "Starsky and Hutch," the captain on "Brooklyn 911" (Andre Braugher), the black female who took over as captain after the black male who preceded her was killed on the ABC show, "Castle." How about the captain in the movie, "21 Jump Street" (played by Ice Cube), and so on. No matter what status, the black man is seen as a punk or sissy, someone to be ignored, disrespected or disregarded. And in some cases they *deserve* to be treated this way.

And what of religion, which is indeed political and black preachers are a joke, to put it mildly. Simply turn your TV to one of those religious shows and watch the likes of Joe Price, Creflo Dollar, TD Jakes and others moon walking all over the stage, sweatin' like stuck pigs and hollering at the top of their lungs. Then down the volume on your television - laughs for days! Who said vaudeville was dead?

In recent years even white comedians make fun of them. They are greedy down to the last dime, the congregation knows it and allows it to take place. From sissies like Eddie Long in Atlanta and effeminate idiots like T.D. Jakes in Dallas, to money grubbers like Joe Price, there is a long tradition of black preachers making money and then engaging in sexual behavior of all types, including the very homosexual behavior that they claim to oppose and that their Bible admonishes with statements like, "Man shall not lay with man."

Then there's these queer-acting black athletes. What else is there to say. Aided by effeminate announcers like Stephen A. Smith ("First Take"), and a host of white boys whose homoerotic responses and descriptions of black athletes clearly show they have issues (by choice), the black man's concept "metro male" would render him a faggot if he did this shit 20 years ago.

When I lived in Dallas, it must have been around 2011, I saw Marcellus Bennett, this huge Black man who plays tight end for the Dallas Cowboys, make one of the most humiliating commercials I've ever seen. If he's not gay then he's damn sure on the verge of becoming that way.

It's a pizza commercial, I believe it was for Papa Johns. Rich Dallas Cowboy owner Jerry Jones has called in and ordered one for himself and his old pals. In comes Bennett, with a blonde wig and a dress, begging for a piece of the pizza. Jones looks at him, realizes who it is, and then shouts "Marcellus!" Bennett is lucky that this commercial was probably only aired regionally. They later traded (or sold) this Uncle Tom to the New York Giants.

Then there's the imagery that pro basketballer Blake Griffin has been signed on to depict and project in his sales of Kia automobiles. After jumping over one of the cars to win the 2011 slam dunk contest, he began making a series of Kia commercials that, on some level, made him appear soft and in some cases, outright homoerotic.

The commercials began with some trips to the past where he visited a young Blake back at his home. Sitting in the garage pushing weights so he could get stronger, he tells his younger self to keep working out and all will be well. Innocent enough. The next one is a slightly older Blake, in the park, again seeking advice. The kid spots the Kia parked on the street next to the park and if it's a space ship. The elder version of Griffin answers that no, it is not, and then begins giving the child more tips, the last one being, "stop wearing jean shorts."

Next is Blake, wearing a jet pack, vertically flying around someone's living room. in a vest and tight suit pants. He's floating around, obviously not being able to control or steer the jet pack. He smashes up the living room as he promotes the Kia automobile. The key was his buffoonish demeanor and tight fitting clothes, looking like every bit of a fag.

Then in typical fashion of the white advertising manipulators. the next several commercials feature Blake with "30 Rock" actor Jack McBrayer. In these, Blake is a super hero, clad in red tights and Jack is his sidekick. In the first one Blake descends (he can fly) to the ground to rescue some white woman. Jack tried to and falls on his ass. Both of them looking as if they are a gay duo.

In an even more homoerotic sequel, Jack and Blake are riding a rope across two high buildings to make some kind of rescue. But if Blake can fly, then why the high wire act? Jack is on Blake's back, but is also riding his ass, as he holds on for dear life.

Then come the absurd commercials exploiting current movie genre and this society's love for war. The first one is Blake behind the wheel of a Kia, on the deck of a battleship getting ready to "fly" off into a war maneuver. After he's informed that he's on a runway, Blake boldly tells the officer, "If I don't come back alive, make sure you tell Emily …" He is cut off by the director of the movie, who tells him he needs a plane, not a car. Blake talks about how powerful the Kia engine is, it has high performance and that the Kia "can fly" and prepares to take off. Before he does he says, "Let's bake this cake!"

Another war-related movie set, this one back in the days of the Romans, finds Blake shooting a movie, surrounded by a large Roman army marching into war. Blake blares out, "My brothers, today we fight for our honor!" The director of the movie shouts, "Cut, cut!" and asks, "Where is your chariot? Blake standing in the front seat of a Kia and looking through the sunroof, tells the director "There is no finer ride in all the land. My Optima has aggressive styling!" Blake adds, "Look man, I didn't come here for a history lesson. I'm here to win!!" He points his sword and leads the hordes into battle, shouting, "To victory!"

What the fuck???

You know, they call the magazine "GQ" and they claim it stands for 'gentleman's quarterly." But in my book, it stands for "Gay man's quarterly." The covers featuring men with no hair on their chests, expensive suits, and the contents inside include articles on "men's health" with on-going references to penis length, sexual prowess and so on. Far too many black athletes and entertainers read this magazine and if they were offered a chance to be on the cover, they'd jump at it. In fact, just recently during an August 19 airing of "First Take," Stephen A. Smith was posturing and primping as usual, and after insulting co-host Skip Bayliss' shirt, made a plea to "appear on the cover of GQ magazine." In his case it might be most fitting.

It is my belief that a lot of brothers who are celebrities and high visibility negroes are on the downlow and simply use marriage and "dating" these beautiful women as a cover. Look at Chris Bosh. When he got "sick" in 2015 and had to miss the last half of the season for the Miami Heat, the first thing that came to my mind was HIV/AIDS. They called it a blood clot on his lungs. Bullshit. When he got sick there was NO TALK of a comeback or his getting well. That's how they treat HIV patients, man! I don't give a fuck if he has three daughters and a wife: if a muthafucka is playing pro ball and is on the road most of the year, he can take it up the ass or suck dick and the bitch at home would never know. And even if she did know, a lot of these bitches will take gettin' paid in exchange for shuttin' the fuck up about her gay husband.

Isaiah Thomas, one of my favorites, talks like a fag. And weren't he and Magic Johnson best pals at one time? And didn't they use to hug and kiss before game when Detroit played the Lakers? And didn't Magic come down with HIV? And wasn't Isaiah the first one to come out against him? And isn't Isaiah on record with women pretty much that of a misogynist, having been sued for sexual harassment when he was an administrator with the Knicks?

The white man knows who's a fag and who isn't, and that's the control that he has over them. He has photos and videos and as soon as they get drafted into the

NFL or the NBA, there are people who are assigned to follow most of them and keep them "out of trouble" – the way you would do a child. One newspaper article, one TV "special report," that is negative, and the white man will do them like they did that young brother from Missouri, Michael Sams, who called himself "coming out." Even with all that football talent, and the fact that he was voted the Most Valuable Player in his college's conference, he was ignored. It didn't help that he was shown tongue kissing his white boyfriend on national television.

The Cowboys pretended to give a shit about Sams and brought him in. But they let him go after the publicity died down. As quiet as it's kept, Dallas is a city full of fags (and dykes), white and black, and keeps their shit on the downlow. He's now gone to Canada to play his game and he might feel more comfortable in those confines since I see a lot of Canadians as having French roots, and I consider French men to be gay. As for the bruthas, the ones I think are fags or on the downlow are not athletes and celebrities, but also politicians and preachers.

Today's Black man is but a shell of his former self. And we have to deal with the issue of AIDS when we talk about this man-on-man sex (downlow) thang. AIDS is killing Black folks.

In Douglas County, where 90% of the blacks in Nebraska reside, 40% of all new AIDS cases are Black women. My theory is that with all the black boys and men being locked up, many of them are having sex with each other while behind bars. That is one place where the HIV virus can be contracted.

The fact is, with such sexual confusion going on, no sane race of people can survive for long. Almost five years ago, the following information gave rise to yet one more nail in the coffin of sisters everywhere. The concept of "the down low" finally crawled out of the quiet of the closet and hit the mainstream. One report from a July 2004 document put it this way:

> Men who have sex with men *and* women are a "significant bridge for HIV to women," the CDC's … data suggest. The findings come in a presentation to the XV International AIDS Conference in Bangkok by CDC researcher Linda Valleroy, PhD. The CDC's Young Men's Survey shows that about one in 10 men reporting sex with men also has sex with women. And more than one in four of these bisexual men has unsafe sex with both kinds of partners (DeNoon & Smith, 2004).

Those poor sister-dykes. How much more endangered can you be when *the male of your own species is killing you off by having sex with other males and then bringing disease home to you?* Wasn't it bad enough when he was screwing women down the block and then giving you some STD or a yeast infection?

Continuing:

"Men who also had sex with women had similar levels of
HIV and STDs [as exclusively homosexual men] and higher
levels of many risk behaviors … Another study presented at
the AIDS conference -- based on interviews with nearly
2,500 bisexual men by the San Francisco Department of
Health -- shows that 14% of men who have sex with men
also has sex with women. But the study, led by Willi
McFarland, MD, PhD, suggests that these men may have
fewer risk behaviors than exclusively homosexual men
(DeNoon & Smith, 2004).

What is a "bi-sexual," anyway? I'm not here to argue one side or the other,
but I will repeat what I've written earlier: if you're a man, either you like sex with
women or you like nuts slamming against your forehead. I can't see a situation
where you could dig both. Maybe I'm just old school, but that's how I view it. And
for that reason, I view this "bi-sexual" thing as just one more fad that we followed
the Anglo off into – along with wife-swapping, shacking up, and a host of other
sexual tendencies that we, today, simply pawn off as "the American way of life."

We are in trouble. Younge (2004) sums things up as he cogently contends
that, "The situation, some argue, is compounded by an apparent scarcity of
potential black male partners, particularly among the middle classes, which can
contribute to black men having a higher turnover of relationships. It also puts more
pressure on women to have unprotected sex. … Many of the women on campus
are panic stricken because of the feeling of scarcity," … "I see a lot of problematic
sexual decision-making among black women across class and age lines." Hence,
the proliferation of the sister-dyke, the perfect survival mechanism.

It's not only on campus: black women are panic stricken because there is
definite scarcity of black males in the society at large! And even with that scarcity
we still have some black men who have such serious psychological issues that they
are leaving the warm confines of a home with a beautiful black woman and
walking down to the corner to get their knob slobbed on by a dude???How could a
black man who already has the benefit of being outnumbered by sisters sometimes
ten to one in our major cities, still want to have sex with a man? If you have those
kinds of yearnings, I don't care what you say, how many women you've got or
what kind of excuse you make: *you're gay in my book.*

What else could you be? Moving right along:

Black men call it the DL: the down low. Fearing loss of
community support, men living this lifestyle keep their
bisexuality -- and their sexual relationships with other men --
secret from their female partners. Whether they call it the DL

or not, many white and Latino men also keep their sexual affairs with men secret from their female sex partners."Most people believe this is only something happening with black men," CDC scientist Greg Millet, MPH, tells WebMD. "We see it in Latino and white men, too. They say they are heterosexual but report sex with other men in the last three months, in the last year, in the last five years. Sexual identity is not destiny" (DeNoon & Smith, 2004).

I know what I think about it. I think men have had these feelings for a long time and those feelings scared the hell out of them. With the coming of sex role socialization, it was even more imperative to hide your feelings of homosexuality. Every male-dominated culture saw a man as acting one way when it came to sex and sexuality, and the Anglo didn't want to feel left out, so he had to "out-macho" everybody else; hence, his proclivity for killing, for guns and especially the hand-held pistol that looks a lot like the male penis – and so on. And the key, of course, to showing total control by all men it seems is to inferiorize the female.

One article quotes an expert on the subject:

John Peterson, PhD, professor of psychology at Atlanta's Georgia State University, has studied the issue for a long time. "The DL is a new name for an old issue," Peterson tells WebMD. "Bisexual men not telling their female partners about their male relationships takes place across all races and ethnicities. But what we really don't know is how these men behave when they have primary male or female partners."

So it's becoming even more difficult to know who the players are. You've got the sister-dyke on one side and the down low brother on the other. This is the *real* definition of Transformers! At one time she had to watch her man chase after every other woman on earth, and now she's got to even be cognizant of his chasing after other dudes! But as the article on WebMD points out, "Secret affairs put the unwary partner at risk of HIV and STDs. But there are different levels of risk. Not all sex behaviors carry the same risk of spreading HIV … We found a long time ago that two-thirds of the time, the female was not aware of the extracurricular sex the behaviorally bisexual man was doing."

What I am finding out from the streets and the sisters who confide in me is that these black men are the very ones who have to define their manhood in ways that put them above suspicion. I recently saw an episode of "Law and Order SVU" where the issue was black men on the downlow. What that episode pointed out were these macho football players who were well-to-do and, once a week, they'd go to one guy's house to "play cards." Of course, you know what they were really doing with each other.

Admittedly, I don't know that much about these rump roasters and switch hitters. All I know is that this country has polluted the morals of almost all of its citizens, and the Catholic Church, the most powerful and richest of them all, is but one prime example. And it seems to trickle down from there.

Look at how money and conspicuous consumption drives black folks mad. They become sexually locked into all kinds of materialism and with all that swag and gaudy jewelry comes freakishness. Of course the people who control the Hollywood casting couch may be gay (not bisexual) themselves, and the people who get the roles might just be going along in order to get along. A lot of the wealthy brothers and sisters are still in the closet because they know that such behavior still carries a stigma in the eyes of their parents and the church they might still attend. But most of us know who's a bone collector, a 'roid riveter, a fudge packer -- and who is not.

But in point of fact, I believe this down low behavior is contributing to the rise of AIDS among black folk. That includes, of course, black women. According to one source, "Most black women with HIV say they were infected through heterosexual contact, but it isn't known how their male partners were infected -- by sex with other men, or by using contaminated needles to inject drugs." I say its sex with brothers who have been locked up, get out of prison after screwing other dudes in the ass for years, and hook up with some woman who sees "he got as nice body." The definition of down low depends on who does the defining.

According to the *Urban Dictionary* (on line), the term comes from the world of hip-hop and R&B music, where it means an illicit relationship. As adapted by a subculture of black men, being on the down low describes men who have sex with other men but appear straight, have relationships with women, and don't acknowledge being gay or even bisexual.

The term doesn't come from hip-hop, either. The *application* of the term does. For instance, the term "pig" refers to an animal, but it wasn't until Bobby Seale's attorney, Beverly Axelrod, used the term in reference to Oakland cops that it caught on. In like manner, the "downlow always meant keeping something quiet, on the hush-hush. " (In fact, the term is used repeatedly by Danny DeVito in the movie "L.A. Confidential"). The hip-hop generation, getting things ass backwards as is their legacy it appears, took the term and gave it the application that we are now discussing: referring to black men who have sex with other men.

Again, we find that the black man is aiding and abetting in the proliferation of the problem; his ego is at stake and he's infected but not willing to tell anyone. Johnson (2005) capsulizes the situation rather nicely when he writes,

> Many down low men find it difficult to see themselves as gay
> because of the stigma attached to homosexuality in the black
> community, said Phil Wilson, executive director of the Black
> AIDS Institute in Los Angeles. Being gay risks rejection by
> family and friends. They don't identify with gay culture,
> which they see as white and effeminate. And when they do
> venture into gay communities like San Francisco's, which are
> predominantly white, they feel unwelcome, according to
> several studies of gay men of color. Because these men have
> so much at stake in keeping their sexual activity secret, it is
> unknown how many there are and it is difficult to trace the
> sexual history of their female partners. The longer these men
> lead double lives, health officials say, the higher the risk for
> their partners.

This doesn't make sense to me. To begin with, these down low men claim to find it difficult to see themselves as gay because of the stigma attached to homosexuality. So then, if there was no stigma would these guys still find it difficult? This is the kind of "if-she-don't-know-it-won't-hurt-her" bullshit that is killing black women; he's afraid for HIS reputation and feelings, but that doesn't stop him from playing hide the baloney pony with his buddy down the street or "around the world in 80 ways" with some guy he barely knows. Absurd!

Moreover, the preceding passage says, "being gay risks rejection by family and friends." Maybe so, but that's a risk that a real man ought to be able to take. If people don't accept you, then that says more about them than it does about you – they prove, by their response and actions, that they never were friends in the first place. Perhaps this is easier said than done, but I have found that it is always better to work with hard facts (no pun intended) than to play with pleasant, but unproductive, dreams.

The excerpt claims that down low men have "so much at stake in keeping their sexual activity a secret." So then they keep it a secret and place all that pressure on the back of the unwary black woman. What cowards! The inability to deal with personal issues (while opting to lead out in public, and talk into any microphone that gets poked in your face), is one reason why black women are being threatened by their own racial mate. Take note of the following series of copouts by so-called "black men:"

> "And what benefit do men have for disclosing their
> bisexuality in a society where positive support and affirming
> resources for bisexual men are all but non-existent, and
> negative stereotypes prevail? This is another example of an
> ongoing debate between public health and public morality.
> Sexual risk behavior is a public health issue; disclosure of

> sexual behavior is, in large part, a personal and moral issue"
> … (Dodge, 2008).

> … [B]lack bisexual men have been largely blamed for the
> high rates of HIV among heterosexual black women. "There
> are bisexually active black men who are contributing to the
> epidemic in the black community, but there are also
> heterosexual men and women, and homosexual men who are
> contributing." (Dodge, 2008).

The on-going debate should be taking place between those black men and the nearest psychologist, first of all! If you want to get some head from another guy, why involve the sister? Tell her up front that you're a rump roaster, a peter puffer or a cock-jockey, and be done with it! According to Dodge, in 2001, the CDC issued a report citing rising rates of HIV and AIDS among gay black and Latino men. The agency then found signs the disease was spreading more broadly among male and female blacks:

> -- In 2002, African Americans accounted for more than half of
> new HIV cases reported in the United States, though they are
> only 13 percent of the population.
> -- In 2003, African American men accounted for 44 percent of
> new AIDS cases among all men.
> -- In 2003, African American women accounted for two-thirds
> of new AIDS cases among all women. White women accounted
> for 15 percent and Latinas 16 percent.
> -- The rate of HIV and AIDS was 58.2 cases per 100,000 black
> women, and only 2.9 per 100,000 white women. The rate for
> Latinas was 8.1 per 100,000.
> -- The leading cause of HIV infection among African American
> women in 2002 was heterosexual contact, followed by injection
> drug use, according to the Centers for Disease Control and
> Prevention.

The black man needs to get his life together and stop trying to adapt to everyone except for the black woman. If a black man wants to live his life as an ass wrangler, a pole smoker or a fudge packer, then he should just go ahead and do it. Why jeopardize someone's mother, someone's sister, someone's grandmother or aunt? Why spread that stuff all over a community that is already dying from more preventable diseases and afflictions than any other race? Why "man," why???

And let me close this section on this black "metro male" (the new homosexual) on two essential notes.

First, remember that if the white man can't buy a "negro," he can sure rent one. And in this case, the black man can be effeminate and continue to act like a bitch, or he can go to prison and be replaced by – you guessed it, the Middle Eastern male, the Arab-American, the Pakistani-American and so on. After all, they're brown (some are darker than us) and they have something in common with the demi-god white boy: they don't like black people born in America any more than he does. And they resent being confused with us, but then again based on what I just described, who would?

Secondly, even though the black man has been "bitchified" (metro male, bitch – what's the difference) and the black woman has been masculinized (the "sister-dyke"), the sex roles will be even more intense because of the inherent psycho-social conflicts. How can a man respect or be attracted long-term to a woman who is always pissed off or threatens to kick his ass or call the cops every time he steps out of line. The bitch in him is going to demand that he be respected and the sister-dyke ain't havin' it. The white bitch of yesterday is also more aggressive and will come to realize that a big dick don't mean nothing if it's attached to a man who is prettier and prissier than she is.

The black man has curlers in his hair, is wearing earrings and all kinds of jewelry, walking around in what they call "skinny jeans" (leotards in my book) and is acting more like a bitch than ever before. Those who are in prison come out and may be more interested in being fudge packers and rump roasters than they are in returning to chasing females who many of them blame for putting them in prison in the first place.

And while we're on the subject of getting arrested, this quasi-homosexuals have no problem putting weed, bags of cocaine, money and other objects in the cracks of their asses. Seriously! They don't hesitate, which means that their asses are always open and ready for business. Whether it's "hide the drugs" business or "monkey business" is up to you to decide. I'm just telling you that these 'metro males' are some weird dudes and once they've been locked up, who knows how they may come out. Republican Presidential candidate Dr. Ben Carson may be gone a little overboard when he said that prison turns men into homosexuals, but I'll say this: he ain't *that* far overboard!

As of September 1, 2015, CNN is airing a show called, "Fresh Dressed," where a bunch of downlow metro niggas are talking about the association between making money and dressing "fresh." People like P. Diddy, Pharrell Williams and several others, looking like bitches, giving out tips on how to dress. Williams even had the nerve to say that you want to "dress like you're free."

In fact, CNN promotions is telling viewers to "join the revolution of fashion through hip hop" by tuning into "Fresh Dressed." Revolution of fashion? It's a "revolution" alright: these asshole millennials are erasing the line between male and female fashion and now dudes dress like bitches and the bitches dress like guys. What's that's the "revolution," and the beneficiary of this bullshit is the demi-god who is making the decisions about what both genders wear, how they act, and what they deem to be "cool."

During an interview about "Fresh Dressed" (plugged as a CNN film) Chris Witherspoon, the editor of Grio.com (September 3, 2015), informed the interviewer was told by Witherspoon (who appears to be a rump roaster himself) that, "guys are owning their own design labels" and that "It's the clothing but also the swagger. These clothes communicate -- the way they dress is kind of like telling their story," Witherspoon says.

Next these fudge packers and effeminate metro males will be getting into hair dressing and salon ownerships.

Add to this list the likes of Usher (Raymond), Nelly, Rev. Eddie Long, and a host of others, and it is clear to see that these are the future generations of black males, folks: talking a lot of macho shit, claiming to be "from the streets," even acting as if or singing about God, but apparently taking it up the ass in the privacy of their mansions and hotel room suites.

And remember, the mothers of these black men are going to accept them whether they're sissies or not. Indeed, these women played a small part if molding them into being the punks and self-centered "mitches" (male bitches, as coined by comedian Kevin Hart) in the first place: spoiling the, ironing and washing their clothes, bailing them out of jail, referring to them as "pretty boy," "lady killer" and the like as they grow up, allowing them to run game on females as they become older, and so on. How can you not grow up to be a bitch when you're treated like one? How can she (the mother) raise a boy to be a man when the dudes she went out with beat her ass, took her money and treated her like shit? A traditional "man" is the last thing she wants her son to be – so she transforms him into a bitch.

And speaking of some seriously aggressive females, let's deal with the white female or, as I call her, the "woMAN."

CHAPTER 3:
The White WoMAN as Action-Oriented Birth Machine (New Black Woman)

She's formerly the societal Barbie Doll, the woman who is pursued and being kissed on by every man on earth. Because of the pervasiveness of this mythology, even the ugliest white bitch believes that the world is her oyster because she has been programmed to think in utopian terms. And this bitch is angry. The lyrics from the song "Fight Song" by Rachel Platten may well sum it up:

> This is my fight song
> Take back my life song
> Prove I'm alright song
> My power's turned on
> Starting right now I'll be strong
> I'll play my fight song
> And I don't really care if nobody else believes
> 'Cause I've still got a lot of fight left in me

Does it sound like this bitch is bullshittin'?

And there may be yet another reason for this rise in "mannishness:" on October 23, 2015 Gloria Steinem was a guest on the "CBS Morning Show." She stated at that time that because of the growing militarization of the world over the decades, for the first time, there are more males than females on earth.

Could there be a concerted effort at "accidentally bombing" and otherwise killing females during war and other crises? And what about the proliferation of both heart disease and breast cancer with men claiming to care so much that they are sporting the color pink, even during football games? Perhaps there is. But knowing this, we can now better explain and understand this change in "sex roles" and why increasing numbers of women have decided to "go it alone" when it comes to associating with or marrying the male of the species.

For the most part, the white woman has been brainwashed to believe that her whiteness, aided in a number of ways by numerous man-made "tools" are intended or designed to make her appear as something that she is not. Following are just a few of what I perceive as being the white woman's "tricks of the trade."

There are tons of cosmetics ranging from Maybelline, Revlon, Estee Lauder, Cover Girl, Avon and Mary Kay to Alberto-Culver, Clinique, Helene Curtis and Max Factor. All aimed at helping her to paint her face, patch holes in her skin, lighten or darken her hair, enhance her eyes and so on. It's the demi-god's way of telling her that he's not satisfied with the way she looks and by complying, it's her way of telling him that she'll purchase the goods and use them, but she's doing it so that she can eventually seduce him, take control of his family, and then take over his role as someone who wants to rule the world.

She takes care of herself physically for the most part. Even now there is a product being advertised called SeroVital, which is nothing short of a human growth hormone, an "amino acid complex." A blonde white woman named Kym Davis, claiming to be a "beauty expert," (and claims to be 56 years old) sings the praises of this product, and women can get it through the mail. It will help her reduce body fat, reduce the appearance of wrinkles and enhance energy. It boosts your HGH "naturally" and sells for $99 in stores. They shoot it up and it gives them energy and "restores vitality." This white woman, despite being a woMAN, is not cutting short her role as seductress.

And there's something for the hair. Daisy Fuentes, an Anglo looking Latina, promotes a product called SecretExtensions gives "even more volume" to the hair and makes it appear longer than it really is. Made of a a keratin conditioned fiber that enables you to wave it around – like the white girls do. You can wash, trim and straighten your SecretExtensions. Now, in vintage white girl fashion, these women can flip their hair, flash it when they turn their heads and so on. Black women, white women and Latinas are going crazy over this style and the hair extensions business is a billion dollar a year industry.

Then there are the numerous types of brassiers, from the U-Plunge, the convertible bra and the full cup to the srapless, the push up and the under wire – all geared toward doing something to her breasts. He also has training bras for the young girls so, at an early age, they can get trained in the purchase of these "aids" that will comply with what he has established as "female norms."

There's the panty shield and panty liners, underalls (to give the appearance that she has an ass) and he even has an operation called a labioplasty, where he can remove the skin covering the clitoris and entrance to the vagina. It's for women who experience pain when they are having sex. I refer to this operation as a "pussy lip adjustment." Speaking of lips, the set on her face are also under cosmetic control (in terms of manufacturing and sales) by the demi-god. Not only has he trained women to wear that lip stick like a badge of honor, but he's developed this shit called Revita-Lift Volume Filler that, like spackle, helps this bitch improve the flaws on her pale face.

Then there are the eyes. There are colored contact lenses (in September of 2015 Air Optix aired a commercial for colored contact lenses promising, "create a beautiful look that works for you …it looks natural"), and even dark women are seeking to walk around with blue, green and hazel eyes. And let us not forget the numerous forms of plastic/cosmetic surgery: Botox, the face lift, the breast augmentation, the beast reduction, the tummy tuck, the buttock lift, the breast life and the Jewish female favorite (usually at the age of 16 as a "gift"), the rhinoplasty (nose job). In many cases cosmetic surgery will get her the man of her dreams (translation: a rich one) and she can live that white picket fence (or gated community) lifestyle that will, in turn, make her the envy of her siblings and the apple of mommy and daddy's eye.

And to make sure that she dresses the part of a slut, male-run companies are making a killing: there's the Wonder Bra, Spanx, Frederick's of Hollywood and Victoria Secret. All this for men who jump on her and get a nut in about 45 seconds. But it's the thought – and the bank book – that count.

And another point that people don't seem to notice is her cartoon-like voice. Have you ever heard them talk? It seems like the more intelligent they are, the more like children they sound. There are articles about blondes and one of the things they describe are their narrow noses and their almost childlike thought patters. Could this be true? Based on my observations from intelligent blondes like Hillary Clinton, Meryl Streep, Greta van Sustrun, Barbara Stanwyk, to the sheer idiocy of Paris Hilton, Heidi Klum, Marilyn Monroe, Cheryl Tiegs, Joy Behar, the Bush twins, and so many more, they sound like wind-up robotic dolls. But they don't have to be blonde to have that silly voice: what about Sarah Palin, Tina Fey, Fran Drescher, and almost every white female news anchor.

In spite of all these physical attributes that lend themselves to a "false femininity, it does indeed appear that image has changed in recent years, and this sex kitten has become more assertive, more confrontative, more crass and in doing so, has become the new white man.

A case in point is this bitch Kendra Wilkinson-Baskett and her reality show, "Kenda On Top." She's married to this guy who looks black named Hank Baskett. They've got three little kids together and this bitch acts like she's single. She talks to him like he's a bitch, she texts other guys, got caught kissing another guy and it was all over the internet. Lives in this mansion, and this guy doesn't seem to get the hint. "Even just a 'hey' from another guy from my past turns me the fuck on," she said during one episode. In another segment she said, "This whole traditional thing bores the shit out of me." In short, this blonde, blue-eyed skank "has it all" and this is the prototype. Her marriage is in trouble and she doesn't give a fuck.

Show after show this bitch wines, cries and spills her guts to her white friends. When she doesn't have makeup on, she looks like shit. She talks about being bored and wonders why she laughs about serious things. She laughs right in her husband's face. She explains that when she was in London she felt free and had gun. And when she got back to the States, the times got "dark." This bitch is a party girl who intentionally set this well-to-do brutha up with three kids. She has a nanny and claims to love the kids. Now she's seeing a psychiatrist, Dr. Shahbaznia. He had an affair back in the day and she hasn't forgotten it. She claims her intentions are not to hurt Hank, but she keeps doing it.

Why? Because she has a reality show and the more conflict, the higher the ratings. This is one side of the new white bitch: open marriage and open legs.

On the flip side of this control freak we find the more aggressive and physically confrontative style. For instance, what else would make a martial arts fighter like Rhonda Rousey talk about fighting boxing champion Floyd "Money" Mayweather? Why else would these white women be given all these super-aggressive television and movie roles where not only do they out-duel men, but they show that they don't need them? Why else would lesbian behavior like women-on-women kissing and sex be getting more and more popular? The white woMAN is taking over the role formerly occupied by the white male, as he moves up to the status of "demi-god."

Even now in summer of 2015 commercials are being aired for Contenelle toilet paper, convincing white women to "go commando." This means walk around with no draws on (as if pussy, even with panty shields and douche, didn't already have odor-related issues). Even now they're selling lingerie on television through a website called AdoreMe.com, where these women can order bras and panty sets. All designed to promote the façade of femininity when, in reality, they are really woMEN just as the black woman is the Sister-Dyke.

Anyway, they call it "girl power" as they break records and accomplish various "firsts," but I don't see these bitches as "girls." I don't see them as traditional women either. They know what they're doing, they have game, they don't have much respect for males and they're out for themselves. Hence, my new term for her: woMAN.

Not only is she the new Black woman in spirit (certainly not in soul), she tans her skin, has makeup to make sure that she stays brown, has Underalls to simulate having an ass, has pushup bras galore, gets her lips injected with collagen so she can have the perpetual "pouty mouth," steals urban language so she can sound hip, and practices all she can so that she can convince people she can dance.

The fact is, she has always been the (procreative) key to the oppressive system, but in the past her actions may have been more covert. But who was sitting there during slavery? Who was staring out the front door as enslaved blacks worked from "can't see in the morning 'til can't sleep at night" on the plantation? Who was standing there with whitey to block the school house doors and make sure niggas didn't get in? She's always been there to send the boys off to war, and that includes the war against niggas.

Don't get me wrong: she's still white politically, ideologically and culturally. A recent spate of reports on CNN titled, "Trump and Women Voters" proves that some 60% of those polled liked the remarks Trump was making, including the insults aimed at women. These white bitches who want to be black in spirit and skin color, are the new white man with female bodies. No, they are not transgender; they are simply more committed to their whiteness than they are to any "ism."

The white woMAN (spelling intended) is an oppressor in her own right and in many cases, has the law on her side. She's a female physically speaking, but in every other way she has become a vindictive male-oriented oppressor that is serving notice on everyone else in the world. Just as he had James Bond and other womanizers using "dick power" to seduce and control women and get information from them, she has replaced him with "pussy power" and is now doing the same thing to gain power, access to power and information. The white woman is the new white man in temperament, purpose and direction.

In fact, she's being treated as such. As CNN reported on August 19, 2015, women can now be Navy Seals if they meet the requirements. On the same day it was announced that two women had made it through the strenuous Ranger School. Who, but the white woman would dare to be a part of the system where men not only outnumber her, but will harass her and if they think they can get away with it, rape her? She is the new white man in terms of mentality and it's only a matter of time that she matches him in physicality.

Already, she's challenging men in more ways than one. On March 5, 2014, the following challenge was issued by Rhonda Rousey, a white female Mixed Martial Arts champion. Check it out:

> To MMA enthusiasts, there's no doubt Floyd Mayweather would get dumped on his head by any of the male UFC champions. But what would happen if the greatest boxer in the world stepped into the cage with Ronda Rousey? The UFC women's bantamweight champ is the alpha female in a sport that encompasses much more than a punching contest. Kicks, knees, takedowns and submissions—these are all aspects of fighting in MMA in which Mayweather hasn't trained. This would explain why Rousey, an Olympic bronze medalist in judo, nonchalantly told Power 106 FM that she could beat Mayweather in an MMA fight (McElroy, 2014).

Need I say more? These white women are slowly but surely integrating themselves into the jock straps of what was at one time a male domain! And it's not only in the military and sports.

A "female Viagra" pill was approved in August of 2015. This "pink pill" is designed to help improve sexual desire in women, and check this out: unlike Viagra that works on boners and nutsacks, this pink pill works on the woman's "brain" and addresses sexual disorders and dysfunction. Women don't need any pills, man; even the most pathetic of losers among them can gap their legs and engage in sex whenever they want to! But that's not enough; in August of 2015 they started airing commercials to get more men to buy Viagra. The commercial begins with women claiming that they want to "cuddle," but that's not Viagra is for! They want to get you on that couch, get your dick hard and then make sure you bust a nut in them so they can set you up with a pregnancy! The result? Eighteen years of child support, marriage or not!

The fact is, the white woman – the new white man – is paving the way for the "transformation" that I allege exists. And her force and influence, like her options in life and her legs in many cases, are opening wider on a daily basis.

It's about control on all levels. For instance, during a September 24th edition of "CBS This Morning," author Jill Schlesinger stated that women make three-fourths of all household purchasing decisions. She quipped at the end of her interview that, "my mother used to say [in reference to the household division of money] 'what's mine is mine and what's his is mine'. That's the way most women, including black women, have felt about household finances for centuries.

Even now there's a commercial by Experian that shows a blonde plopping her feet on a bank officer's desk (while her husband looks sheepishly on) and informs the bank official that she already knows what her credit score is. The bank officer is amazed at her knowledge, and he agrees to her terms. Then, as she walks out of the building, husband in tow, the narrator continues kissing her ass.

On September 14, 2014, Sen. Kirsten Gillibrand appeared on CBS' "Face the Nation" to talk about her new book, *Off the Sidelines*. What she said and what the book contains buttresses my belief that the white woman is the new white man.

What is she talking about? The white man talks about issues the way he sees them and rarely ever included the white female. Now that he's moved on to "demi-god" status and left the role of white male to her, she's doing the same thing. All of a sudden the struggle is about "women" (and when they say women they mean white women) and how to get more power, be heard, protest and so on. And what is it for? There ain't no black women on their agenda: it's about white women getting more than they've already got. They appear to be just as power hungry as their man is. In both cases they believe that they speak for everyone when they say "we," "us" or "women."

It was at one time referred to as "the old boys network," those fuddy duddies who sat there making decisions that influenced millions of lives. Now he's elevated his status to the level of "demi-god,' and the "old boys network" has become "the white girl's network" because it transcends age. White women from all backgrounds benefit from the fact that they lack skin color (white privilege) and have marketed it into a key to their power. She's the new white man and is not afraid to make it plain: back are the skin bleaching creams that promise to " make your skin clear" while deeming anything dark on your skin as a "blotch," and back are the stockings, bras and undergarments whose color is called "nude" or "flesh" – as if everyone's skin color is the pinkish color of hers. The white man may have created it, but she's marketing and benefiting from it.

In simpler terms, the white woman is calling the shots. For instance, the same lust the white man had for women of color she now has for men of color. Well, she's always had it but because of social conventions, had to keep it to herself. But now, under the guise of being "independent" and "liberated," she can suck all the black dick she wants, give birth to all the mulatto kids she chooses to, and date and flaunt whatever black man suits her fancy. You might call this the "Kim Kardashian Syndrome." She will have no problem picking one up: black men seem to find white women, no matter how ugly, simply irresistible. In simpler terms she can have free sexual choice just like the white man had during slavery. She is, indeed, the new white man.

She no longer needs him for babies. They've got sperm banks all over the place, and she can do whatever she wants to do with those embryos. She has enough financial wherewithal to adopt any child she wants, and in many cases it is a child of color. Perhaps she knows that little white boys grow up to be racist white men and she doesn't want anyone to threaten her power, and she doesn't want to cope with all that excess baggage when little Johnny comes home having gotten his ass kicked for calling someone a "nigger" or a "spic."

At one time such audacity would be viewed as "sassy" or "uppity." At one time she would have gotten her ass kicked for some of the things she's doing – and thinking - today. Go back a few centuries and she would have been lynched or burned at the sake. But social progress has been to her advantage, and the white man, pussy whipped as he used to be, has stood by why she's racked up college degrees, gone to work and earned her own money, and etched out a philosophy of "fuck you" when she feels like it (that is after she puts into motion her "where do you work" approach).

Although the traditional male role included rape and sexual abuse of women, the white woman accomplishes these things without the use of physical force because there are different types of "force" or coercion: there is economic coercion, social coercion, political coercion and ideological coercion. The later serves as the basis for this role she has assumed and for the power, both latent and manifest, that she now exudes and exhibits.

Look at Hillary Clinton. Do you think this pants suit-wearing bitch is going to be any different than her husband was, or for that matter when it comes to black people, much different than either of the Bush's? She talks all that shit about caring about the poor and about "Black Lives Matter," but that's the same shit her husband did. Once he got in office, he apologized for slavery – something he didn't have the power to do, and then proceeded to lock up more black males than anyone before him with that minimum Federal Guidelines shit. Just recently, in June of 2015, he said he was sorry for having voted for that legislation.

According to the August 5, 2014 edition of the "PBS News Hour," half of all advanced business degrees are now going to women. What does that say for the changing of the guard, impact on economy and the action-oriented/man-like superwoman who is white? Two decades ago I charged that the white woman was simply saying scoot over and let me oppress people with you. She wanted to be the white man's assistant in global domination.

But since that time his maltreatment of her, the gap in the pay scale between white men and white women, his on-going trivialization of her prospects and potential have turned her against him. She not only wants to "wear the pants," but she wants to burn the pair he has on – with him in 'em! And remember: those old white bastards who run corporate America are married to white women. Who do you think takes over and inherits the power if she wants to? Who do you think he tells all his secrets do at night while they're in bed? Who gives him children to train to become new racists? "The hand that rocks that cradle rules the throne."

The July 12, 2004 issue of *Newsweek* is one that has generated controversy because of the manner in which the authors dealt with their topic, "The Secret Lives of Wives." According to their bold faced thesis situated above the article after the preface, "Why They Stray," the statement posits that, *"With the workplace and the Internet, overscheduled lives and inattentive husbands – it's no wonder more American women are looking for comfort in the arms of another man."* This "breakthrough" is nothing that men of color haven't known for some time about white women – who are, after all, the numerical majority in this country.

Therefore, I am in full agreement with Darlene Clark Hine when she wrote,

> At no time in our history have we been in greater need of the wisdom, courage and determination of our Black foremothers. Many black communities today exist in a state of chaos, crisis, and conflict. There is no progress without survival, and our survival is currently precarious. However, at the risk of sounding sanguine, I believe there is power in history. To tap the hidden reservoirs of power, we must listen to the voices and look into the lives of the women who have brought us this far. In order to ensure that a new American history includes us all, it is imperative that we look at the face of our past (Hine, 2000: B100).

Maybe the words of the great civil rights activist Fannie Lou Hamer is a good way to end this section of my analysis for all concerned. She once said, "The only thing you have to do that's important in life … is just go on being your own normal, black, beautiful selves as women, as human beings." Because of the conditions we live under, and the precarious situation of most black families. It may well be too late. These black women are imitating the white woman, from the fake hair and the makeup to the fucked up "man-hater" attitudes.

In simpler terms, the white woman cometh ...

<u>Politics</u>

What I refer to as "The politics of "tears and the law" is a weapon that women have come into in recent years. Time was you could slap the shit out of one of them and that was that. But now, with this white woman using her pussy power and expanding it into the political arena, you can't even touch a woman and expect not to go to jail. In fact, they've taken it a step further: find a man they don't like, and then set him up to violate a restraining order or, for that matter, to simply enter the house. And if that house is in her name, she can just let out a scream and when the cops come, point at you and charge assault. And off you go. This is politics in its purest form: having the system at your beckon call.

If fact, many states, including Texas, have a law that if there is a call for a domestic issue, "somebody is going to have to go to jail." Even if the man is the victim, in many cases he will go to jail if it is proven that by protecting himself, he pushed her to keep her away. And now they've come up with a new law, which was described on a September 6, 2015 segment of "Dateline on ID" (the Investigation Discovery channel). It's called, "rape by deception." Women can now claim that they were not forcibly assaulted by were taken advantage of if a man pretends to be someone he's not. That makes all men guilty, in my book! But this is what happens when you concoct a bullshit myth of "the weaker sex" to use as a tool to control a female. She comes back, via the legal system, with a vengeance. "Hell hath no fury like love, to hate, turned."

On another level you can see what happens to the few white women who manage to get elected into the system – they are as callous and cold as their white male counterparts. The likes of Michelle Bachman and Sara Palin, and not to be outdone are Nancy Pelosi, Diane Feinstein and Hillary Clinton. For the most part, hawks draped in doves clothing. That is why I refer to them as "woMEN."

In August and September of 2014 there was a big controversy about "sexism in Congress." This might sound like the white women being feminine and being hurt. But no. It's about a masculinized person who wants a bigger piece of the rock. She's not telling her newly deified mate to slow down; she wants more power and she wants to share it. And it's getting to the point where she wants a larger and larger slice of the white supremacy pie. She wants to be recognized and not treated the way she and her white male mate used to treat black people.

The controversy started with one white Congresswoman charging that there is "sexism in the gym." The gym?? Sexism in the Senate? Kirsten Gillibrand in her book, *Off the Sidelines* documents sexist comments from members of the House. One white man told a white woman, "You're even pretty when you're fat." Another said, "Don't lose too much weight – I like my girls chubby" as this particular member of the Senate squeezed her waist. No woman whose been around there is shocked that it is taking place, according to Gillibrand. On "Meet the Press" the same week the discussion was that the sexism in Congress, is generational. What do these women expect?

At the root of these political antics is the fact that the white woman has come to the realization that when all is said and done, all women need men for is their sperm; impregnate them and the job is done. Many are even refusing child support because, according to these newly "masculinized" white women, men are simply a pain in the ass. And they make a valid point.

The white woman is in control even when the white man trips all over his demi-god status. Take the case of the handling of the Ray Rice case by the National Football League. Rice was suspended "indefinitely," but that was after the league initially only suspended Rice for two games prior to that. Women (read: white women) were appalled and threatened to boycott the League. Roger Goodell, the commissioner of the NFL crumbled and put the male bastion at risk. This demi-god immediately patronized the "new white woMAN" by appointing four white women (read: new white men) to help lead some kind of bullshit commission on "social responsibility." Again: "the hand that rocks the cradle rules the throne" and when it comes to women and their impact on the demi-god's purse strings, "the hand that shakes the pom-pom has the final say."

What about the "politics" of police work?

A woman named Connie Fletcher wrote a book called *What Cops Know: Today's Police Tell the Inside Story of Their Work on America's Streets.* I reviewed it a decade ago (my review was over 250 pages) and following is what Fletcher described based on her interviews with Chicago cops and my interpretation of those findings and how this all relates to the "transformation" that I allege has taken place when it comes to the white woman.

As I wrote, "Moving to the issue of sexism – a twin to the racism that most cops practice, belief in, and work to hide from the white public. Sexism permeates the thinking of every man on earth, but the white man is the one who has institutionalized the degradation of women even in the workplace. That includes criminal justice. Check out what one cop says about his female counterparts:"

> You gotta know when to turn it on and when not to turn it on.
> If you turn it on alt the WRONG time –and there are police
> officers who do that – it escalates things. That's the problem
> with some women police, you know, they want to come on
> and be the hard-ass all the time, they're Jane Wayne, they're
> Dirty Harriet; they think they got something to prove, and it
> ends up just escalating things. It's not good (p. 17).

White women are white first and female second. This may sound harsh, but I make this statement based on their actions. As women first, would they not despise the white man's acts as much as people of color do? As women first would they not expose some of the dirt that he brings home and tells her about? No, she's white first and her job is to work next to "her man" (demi-god) to ensure and maintain white supremacy. She's white first and female second and that's why I alleged that she is the new white man: her "femaleness" is physical only. Read what the cop said in the previous paragraph. Mentally, she is as racist as he has ever been and that's why her children grow up to be racists. Again, "The hand that rocks the cradle rules the throne."

As it relates to the "politics of policing" as I call it, these women are imitating what they see on the street and in the locker room; they imitate what they hear during roll call and it is clear that the more "hard" you are, the more distant you are, the more hate you can show toward "those other people," the more respect you get from the white male. They may have had a father, uncle or brother who was or is a police officer. They feel they must prove themselves and that means being as much like the white male officer as possible.

Besides, most of the female cops are white and they are just as racist as their man is; they cling to the same myths and stereotypes as the white male. The only difference is gender. And some of these women even incorporate the sexist beliefs that the white man has circulated about them (in the same way that some black people suffer from what Dr. Roderick W. Pugh called "adaptive inferiority"). One female cop told Fletcher:

> Women have limitations. I'd be the first to admit it. We're
> not as strong as men. But—as a woman you can do things. I
> remember we were driving through Lincoln Park one night,
> and I was sitting on the lap of one of the guys I work with.
> We were laughing, but we were working. We sat there like
> a couple watching someone break into a car. And he knew
> we were right there; didn't pay any attention to us. I'm
> sitting in my partner's lap. I have my arm around him, and
> I'm talking into the police radio I'm holding behind his

> head … and they moved on the guy. He just thought we
> were a couple sitting there, necking (pp. 30-31).

The only "limitations" women have are the ones that the white man (demi-god) places on them. This thing about strength has long since been offset by the coming of technology (and you can add to that her trickery, shrewdness, and "fuck anybody to get what you want" attitude). The white man knows this. So he works on the self-worth of the woman at all levels. If she wants to be a cop, it begins with the classes she takes where she must study male theories, deal with male teachers and be programmed to believe that justice, whiteness and "maleness" are synonymous.

By the time she reaches the police academy she's in a nearly all-male domain and is treated like a pariah. If she makes it through, she's usually paired with a guy who is trying to fuck her during every minute of down time that they get. That TV shit where the white man and woman are partners and he goes through this "I don't really notice your tits" bullshit is just that: bullshit. In real life, "Law and Order: SVU"'s Elliott Stabler would have screwed the shit out of his partner, Olivia Benson. Rick Castle, the writer who is teamed with detective/cop Kate Beckett would have fucked her much earlier were it real life (as of the writing of this book they are engaged to be married).

If the female cop acts feminine or docile, the white demi god and his cronies will undoubtedly label her a dyke if she resists the advances of these dog-ass male cops.

Look at what the female in the preceding quote was reduced to? Sitting in a man's lap pretending to be making out. What if she was married? What if she had a steady boyfriend? Why does the woman have to act in such a manner? This is what should be addressed, rather than discussions of how many women have assimilated, sold their souls and, as a result of doing both, have been able to make it onto the police force.

If this analysis and response to Fletcher's book doesn't prove anything else, it should prove that ***cops, for the most part, are sick individuals.*** And since the ones who consider themselves sane don't expose the sick ones or work to get them kicked off the force, they are as sick as the culprits are. Therefore, the white woMAN continues the tradition as the white male advances to the status of demi-god.

And a similar method of operation and value system can be found in any system or institution where the white man is in the majority or in charge. And she doesn't complain about it because she wants to share the power.

<u>Popular Culture</u>

The white man's mythology is permeated with machismo and the suppression of the female. So when you see her begin to boss him around, insult his masculinity – even in the realm of his super heroes – you know that she has now assumed a role that dominates what was at one time the white male domain. And she's got a slew of role models paving the way for her. Her image, like her role politically, culturally, socially and intellectually, has been *masculinized.*

There was an old TV show called "Remington Steele." The show was about a woman who wanted to start a private detection agency, but was not being taken seriously because of the fact that she was female. So she found an office space (luxurious of course – money is never an object) and created an illusory character named "Remington Steele." She found just the "type" and hired him. They got plenty of clients because most customers felt that the place was headed by a man. This is much the same as the image and basis for the white family; everyone thinks the man is the head (and their Holy Bible backs this bullshit) when, in reality, she uses pussy politics on a number of levels to wield the *real* control

This, in essence is the gist of the white woman as action oriented superwoMAN; in essence, the new white male. She takes charge of him and orders him around to the point where he has relinquished his male-oriented role and tasks to assume the higher role of demi-god (see elsewhere in this book). She is now a "man" in the traditional sense of the word, although she still retains female body parts and power hungry attitude.

Back in the day on TV there was Barbara Stanwyck, a beauty who got many roles as a leading lady but was a dyke in real life. But the role that set the stage for the white woman as the new white man was her role as Victoria Barkley on "The Big Valley." Her daughter, the ultra feminine Audra did nothing more than purr, but she had three super macho sons: Heath, Nick and Jarrod. But she owned the land, controlled the entire area, and was one of the first women turned man that was hurled at the American public.

The reality is now beginning to manifest itself more regularly in the popular culture, especially the movies. Led by Angelina Jolie and her action roles in movies like, "Salt," "Wanted," and "Mr. and Mrs. Smith," she's paving the "I don't need no man" path for others to emulate, the polar opposite of the 1940s and 1950s when "Donna Reed" and "Ozzie and Harriet" set the stage for female passivity. Not only is this white woMAN the new white man, she's even more vicious than he is: not only does she have the power to "sic" him on whomever she hates, but she has her own secret feminine weapons that enable her to do the crime without really doing any real time.

That's right: like their cowardly white male counterparts the white woman has now taken his place in the realm of being assassins and snipers. An upcoming flick called "Cleaners" features not one, but two female assassins. Let us not forget the aforementioned "Salt," "Lucy," and we cannot forget the hit ABC show from a few years back, "Alias," which starred Jennifer Garner. Along similar lines is "Covert Affairs," which features this blonde named Annie who goes all over the world fucking up men in the name of the U.S. government (art imitating life).

The popular culture projection as the white woMAN as the new white man continues on. How about the CBS program, "The Good Wife," where this woman has all the power and week after week, does what she wants to do no matter what it is. She is no "wife" – she is an intrepid iconoclast that doesn't give a shit about any man, let alone a husband! Even now her power grows as, by October of 2014, she is about to embark on a bid for political office! Today, in a more politically powerful role, CBS is coming out with "Madam Secretary," a show starring Tea Leoni as a secretary of state "with an attitude." During a promo for the show that was aired in August, she's in bed with some guy and she's telling him, "I'm here to make change in the world."

In another promo for "Madam Secretary," as she sashays through her office flipping her blonde hair, one caption reads, "It isn't politics as usual," and a yet another adds, "Defend the nation – by any means necessary." On yet another bravado oriented promo she tells another member of the Cabinet, "I've never met a situation where I don't have a choice in the matter." Finally, while walking down the hall with another official, September 5, 2014 promo for the show has her uttering, "You may have picked up on this, but I'm not big on protocol." Just what this country needs: tits, a short skirt, blonde hair, a menstrual cycle, an attitude and access to the most powerful military in the world!

By November of 2015 the Sunday lineup on CBS, following "60 Minutes" was, as follows: "Madame Secretary," "The Good Wife," and the new "CSI: Cyber," the latter starring Patricia Arquette. Three white women, all aggressive slut-like power brokers.

Not to be outdone, NBC is about to air "State of Affairs" featuring another ultra-powerful blonde, Kathryn Heigl. A promo for an upcoming Marvel comic book spin-of (an eight part series), ABCs "Agent Carter," includes the statement, "Sometimes the best man for a job is a woman." See what I'm saying? She's mastered all the masculine and androgynous behaviors, she clearly wants nothing to do with her white mate, and for the most part, he thinks he's too good for her. The white woMAN is the new white man, plain and simple.

When it comes to popular culture it's not just about the white woman exerting themselves in the political arena. It's also about pussy politics combined with the power that comes with it (ala the Biblical Delilah or history's Mata Hari and Cleopatra). In white America TV shows like "Mistresses," "Scandal" and "Revenge" immediately come to mind. And don't forget the secret agent recruit played by Angelina Jolie in the movie "Wanted," or the international assassin Black Widow of the "Avengers" super hero movie.

Then the popular culture invokes the power of these white women (new white men) as cops. There's a show on the Oprah Winfrey Network (OWN) called, "Police Women of Dallas." Now I lived in Dallas for six years and there's two things about the cops: (1) they're stupid and (2) they don't play around. So I don't know what makes these women so special that they have a show based on their gender, but I know that they can't be much different from the white males because they, like their real male counterparts, seem to have a license to kill, one that they are more than happy to use, especially when it comes to Latinos and Blacks.

All these new wave crime fighting bitches have a "don't take any shit" attitude. The woMAN on the show "Stalkers" is hard core and doesn't give her partner the time of day. We already touched on the female on "Law and Order: SVU" who has risen through the ranks and now with her original partner, Elliott (Chris Melroni) gone, Mariska Hargitay's character Olivia Benson, is large and in charge. The first few years some viewers thought she was a dyke because she was so hard core, but now she's been allowed to adopt a child named Moses (don't worry – he's white) and they've humanized her. But she still has an "I don't take no shit" attitude. The new white male personified.

White women, the new white men, are being inspired by popular culture to embark on power trips and killing sprees and have the same ends and goals as their man used to before his status was self-elevated to the level of "demi-God." Joanna Coles, editor of *Cosmopolitan* magazine, is taking the magazine into the political realm just in time for the upcoming election. On the September 5, 2014 interview on "CBS This Morning," she claimed that, "Sixty two percent of college intake is young women."

Back in the old days you'd see a white woman slap her man and he'd take it like a punk (except for Humphrey Bogart and James Cagney). She would slap anyone knowing that she was getting her point across because such action was presumed to be her "acting out of character" and as a result, you knew she was angry. Not only has this drastically changed where now she will slap the shit out of anyone, but she is now hitting men with her closed fist and kicking him in the balls. It's becoming so common that it's being deemed as "funny." I don't see anything funny about such action in the face of the society myth that "a man should never hit a woman." If a woman hits me, she's gonna get the shit knocked out of her, plain and simple.

In the movie "Thor: The Dark World ," the so-called demi-god is once again united with the woman he loves (a scrawny earth woman played by Natalie Portman). Upon his return to Earth, he locates her and she's supposed to be happy because he's been gone back to his home, Asgard, for a while. After having expressed the fact that she missed him, she turns around and slaps the living shit out of him, not once but twice. He does nothing about it. He even goes so far as to take her back to Asgard with him and she proceeds to be the basis for its near destruction and the death of his (Thor's) mother (she was defending the earth woman when she got killed). Does Thor hold his earth ho responsible? No.

In the movie "Young Guns II," Billy the Kid and his gang are trapped in a building by a evil land baron and the cavalry. As the situation grows more dire, a man who is a supporter of the Kid tells his wife to leave the house and forces her out for her own good. This red-headed white bitch leaves the house and walks up to the leader of the cavalry. She proceeds to slap the living shit out of him and calls him an "animal." He has her taken away, to where we do not know. But I do know this: there was no counter-slap by this man who was a killer (in the name of the United States) which means that the "never hit a woman" message was alive and well on several levels.

In the movie "Wyatt Earp," the Earps have just finished a shootout with the Clanton gang at the OK corral. They're rehabbing in a room with the Earp wives after one of the Earp brothers has been shot. This particular Earp brother's wife turns to Wyatt Earp (the ringleader and deputy) and says, "I wanted him to leave here but he wanted to stay here with you." Then she slaps the shit out of him. Wyatt Earp has just finished gunning down a group of men, he's got a rifle in one hand and his handy six-shooter strapped to his waist. And this bitch slaps him. If that's not "balls," then I don't know what is.

During a September 9, 2014 episode of "The Young and the Restless," this ex-GI green beret type guy named "Stitch" is sitting at the table with Victoria Newman discussing the baby she's carrying – which might be his. As he's talking Victoria's younger sister, Abbie, walks up behind him and cuffs him upside the head – hard. Not one of those staged soap opera slaps, but an actual cuff, the kind that snaps when you do it right. She had just hired him for a job and was "angry" because he was talking to her sister – who represents a competing fragrance company. What did he do? He didn't do shit but stand up and start arguing with her.

In short, *the white woman has no fear of the white man and has taken his place as the oppressor of all she surveys*. I saw one white woman slap the shit out of Bruce Banner, who she knew could turn into The Hulk at any time. Another one is Mystique of "X-Men" fame. She's a shape-shifting villainess who can transform, even assuming male figures, which is probably the ultimate for these new empowered white women: look like a women but when you need to, assume a male appearance in order to dupe the public. Men have been doing it for years: you can hardly name a white male star of any merit who has not gone "drag" in some movie or TV role. And the white man has been getting black men to do it as well;

David Chapelle walked off the set when these peckerwoods tried to get him to put on a dress for a skit. What's wrong with these homoerotic white boys?

In July-August of 2014 Scarlett Johannsen assumed the movie role of "Lucy," some woman that could use almost 100% of her brain (scientists claim that the average human can only use about 10%), and she was wreaking havoc on the scientists that were manipulating her and any other man that stood in her way. Women know they have power, but the white man, who is more committed to and concerned about maintaining control over the world, doesn't give a shit. She rules human beings - he (the white man) rules the planet itself and let him tell it, all of the "known universe."

In September of 2015, a promotion for a new show proves the status of this white woMAN and her new role. The NBC show is called, "Blindspot" and the lead actor, a white woman known only as "Jane Doe" - is billed as "the female Jason Bourne." As part of the promo she is deemed by one of the male officials as "the best chance" for America or something along those lines. Another promo tells us that she cannot remember who she is but then cut to the line where she demands, "I want to see someone in charge!" The perfect white woman: blank slate of a brain, power hungry, aggressive and loaded town with tattoos.

Not to be outdone, ABC is airing "Quantico," about some FBI bitch who is out to look for a snitch inside of the organization. The white woMAN lives! In addition to that little number they have another slated called "Blood and Oil," which pits two white bitches – one who loves her family and another who craves power, both blonde – against one another.

Finally, another example in popular culture and it has to do with the world of sport.

Women learned long ago that men like football and they enjoy watching it. So they boned up on their lingo and learned the game. It was then used as another "tool" to go where the boys are, become one of the gang, and hang around until they can find one who will fuck them. Women are the majority in America so professional sports teams have to tow the line.

The hypocrisy of white folks knows no bounds. So as part of their commitment to "character," sports teams are now concerned about losing fans. So they are passing rules that if you are involved in any domestic violence issues, you (the athlete) will be suspended without pay - meaning loss of hundreds of thousands of dollars -- in some cases, millions. These sports decision makers are also talking about when it comes to drafting players out of college, meaning that if any player has any incidents of domestic violence, then pass him up come draft day because they don't want the female fans on their ass (they spend money on games, too).

Since most of the athletes being drafted are Black males, and since most of them have girlfriends, wives or some kind of significant other, the "deal" that is made, the contract that is extended, has everything to do with how he treats that female -or how she CLAIMS she's treated - and whether or not he's going to make the professional ranks. In most cases she's latched onto him while in college, sucked his dick on a regular basis and put up with his shit – all in preparation for him to turn pro.

If she likes him, has him under control and is in a good mood, then he'll make it. But if he fucks up or she has reported him in the past, right or wrong, if he gets out of line, then he's screwed. In other words these women control the fate and future of the blue chip athlete – during college, during the draft and after he signs the contract. If they so choose, they can *ruin* him.

Does this not mean that the woman is in control? In a sexist society where the man is presumed to be in control of his own life, doesn't this show that SHE is the one in charge? And in fact, based on the way the law is written, hasn't this bitch ALWAYS been in control? Black women – the new white women – have copied the white female's looks and fucked up attitude, but they can't access any real power because of their skin color. But they can roar as if they rule when it comes to the faggotized Black male. And what white women do to the world and to American society, the Black female (the new white woman) does to the black man, every chance she gets.

Under the false veneer of caring about this new and improved white woMAN, professional sports leagues are taking it out on the male athlete. These bitches know what they're doing. They can't whip a man's ass physically, but they sure in the hell will try. Then it court they use their documented evidence that they were simply acting in "self-defense" and that they feared for their lives.

The woman who ran up on Ray Rice knew she couldn't beat him up. What was on this woman's mind? "I'm gonna knock Ray the fuck out?" So she gets her ass kicked (knocked out) and now Rice is fucked. After the incident he went so far as marry the bitch (why, I don't know), and the white male (demi-god) still didn't cut him any slack. Pretending to give a fuck about women's rights, white boys canned Rice's Black ass. Lucky for Rice the woman was also Black - had it been one of those white bitches, he might have gotten life with no chance of parole!

If any one of these women, realizing the pro potential (read: millionaire) status of one of these men, and decides to "get' this guy because they found out that he has another woman on the side, or might have prematurely ejaculated on the pussy one time too many, these women can wreck that man's future. They can have him on his knees begging, "oh please, baby please!" so he won't lose his job, his money and his status. She now has that kind of power. And don't think these bitches are beyond blackmail or bribery: they've been setting men up for centuries with that "you got me pregnant" and "the baby is yours" bullshit. A recent on line article written by a professional prostitute said that up to 25% of married NBA players have been blackmailed at one time or another. So engaging in the actions I just outlined is not beyond their moral compass.

The white woman is taking over, replacing the white man as the world's dominant oppressor. Television cop/detective shows like "Castle" and "Bones" (and more recently "Law and Order: SVU") show the white woman large and in charge and, while falling for the white man, still dominates not only her profession, but also the home life. She is independent and there is never any leeching for bill money and every time they go out, he pays. He has become her ho, her bitch, her willing thrall -- whether he wants to admit it or not. And this brings me to my closing point.

This bitch is taking over with HIS help. There are a number of examples, but let me give you one that I've noticed. In my book, these dating websites and all that shit – it's just an economic engine that this bitch can use to hook this pussy-whipped asshole into financing her future, getting into debt and then when she feels like it, divorce his ass and get half his shit.

Check out how lonely these white men (and their negro lackeys) must be, busily pursuing the woMAN. They've got E-Harmony, Zoosk, and Match.com, just to name the most popular ones. And basically what is it: white men and negroes searching the web for pussy. Some of the sites claim that they are about long-term relationships, but once again, that depends on how good the pussy is. These women can lie and fake orgasms all day long and trick any man into believing that "she's the one." But what is a date in America? For the most part it's the man taking this bitch anywhere she wants to go, and the more expensive, the better. He pays because in America, it's the "gentlemanly thing to do."

And all the while this over-rated, egotistical bitch is thinking of herself. A national commercial aired on TBS is for a new perfume called, "Si." As you know "si" means yes in Spanish. This white bitch tells viewers, "si to life, si to freedom, si to seduction, si to us, si to love" and now, get this: *"si to myself."* And after all when it comes to women in general and these Barbie dolls in particular, isn't this what it's all about?

So he's hunting for pussy, she knows it and she makes him grovel for it. It takes more than one date (one website tells you, "Like comes before love") because in that way she can find out if he has the financial wherewithal to be considered for the long term. If this woman just wants a casual relationship, does this mean that she will pay? Hell no! Oh, some of them will go through the motions and talk that "let's go dutch" shit, but it's a front. The more they pretend that they don't want that man's money the more likely they are to get it.

I include sick negroes on this list as well because there are some left who aren't fags. They do whatever whitey tells them and I would have to say many (most?) of them are cruising the internet looking for white bitches. The word is out that she's weak minded and easy to fuck (most will suck your dick before they'll shake your hand), but that has nothing to do with physical attraction or finding a "match." It has to do with pacification and placation. As long as you pay, that's more money they'll have to stockpile and save it for a rainy day. That's the key to power: long-term thinking. Men are after pussy and power, she's after power, period. Besides, many of them are sucking more pussy than any man could ever hope to. They just keep it on the downlow.

And speaking of licking pussy, let us now turn to the ultimate muff-diver of all time, the white boy.

CHAPTER 4:
The White Man as Demi-God/ Omnipotent Administrator*

In *Soul On Ice*, Eldridge Cleaver coined the term "Supermasculine Menial" to define the black man's relationship to the white oppressor, whom he labeled "The Omnipotent Administrator." I don't believe that the white man is omnipotent, but I do believe that he thinks he is, and is incessantly striving to be. Hence my term "quasi-deity" and "demi-god" because his mythology, if you trace it back, includes a series of creates that were allegedly spawned by "the gods" and yet had one human parent. They were considered "demi-gods." Among these are Thor and Hercules. But notice that both -- along with the Christian God who got the "Virgin Mary" pregnant -- lusted after and impregnated white bitches from Earth. In fact, both Hercules and Thor are the products of such unions when their fathers screwed Earth bitches. Just wanted you to know

In my view, far too many people in American society -- "deify" the police. To "deify" someone -- or in this case to deify an entire class of people or an institution -- means, "to make a god of; to look upon or worship as a god." Also, "to glorify, exalt, or adore in an extreme way; idolize." Deserving or not, this society deifies the white man, who is in charge of all institutions in this country.

The white man's "demi-God status" (as a group or collective) is represented by his military power (force of arms), his media (pro-white propaganda) and his ability to manipulate his legal system. When it comes to military power his bombs (the power of near total destruction), his aircraft (drones, jets, guided missiles), his tanks (ground power) and of course his guns and military orientation enable him to inflict pain and fear on the majority of the world's peoples.

His media dominates the world, and this includes the Jewish media control of newspapers, film, television and even radio. His laws change from day to day, and always in his favor. He can torture, imprison, alienate, deport, ostracize, impoverish and virtually control every human being in this country. At the same time, he continues to glorify and elevate himself so that he becomes the self-proclaimed expert in every field of study.

And there is another element of this "demi-god" status that has always existed but is becoming more prominent through the white man's politics and popular culture: *his obsession with creating life and controlling it.*

Even back during the days of his pseudo-science obsessions, the white man was concerned about the genitals, skin color and biology of people of color. His scientists were cutting up human bodies and coming to conclusions that black men had black sperm. He claimed that the cranial capacity of the skull was an indicator of intelligence or lack thereof. He dogged out Italians and claimed that their olive colored skin was an indicator of their tendency toward criminality. He wanted to define life and then he went on to literally create it.

The story of "Dr. Frankenstein" is a metaphor for what this self-proclaimed demi-god has done all over the world. He has created forms of life through psychological programming and he has even gone so far as to master the science of "cloning." He has genetically engineered farm animals so that they can become bigger and as a result, more marketable. He has done the same thing with plants and in his gardens so that they could reap larger harvests. And in the process of doing these things he knowingly realized that whatever serum he shoots into these animals and plants and whatever pills he gives to members of the kingdom of thingdom are going to be digested and ingested by HUMAN BEINGS!

This in turn has created an entire race of children who are growing too fast, whose minds are not as mature as their bodies, boys with body hair and girls with breasts. This is a form of genetic engineering that is not being dealt with; those in the social sciences simply want to deal with the OUTGROWTH or RESULTS of this stuff: kids screwing up in the classroom, more anger among the members of the population, and so on. And down the road the little girl with the 36-inch breasts and the boy who is 7-feet tall can be pimped in beauty pageants and the porn industry as well as professional sports, respectively. The demi-god is, without a doubt, responsible for this shit.

Politics

To begin with, even in his status as ultimate ruler or demi-god, he still retains some homosexual tendencies, similar to those imposed upon the black male. The white man's history and tradition are filled with examples of homosexuality, from his rulers in ancient Rome to his poets and politicians in ancient Greece. He seems to have always been gay or "gay curious." .

Even during slavery he not only had sex with black women, but also took liberties by sodomizing the black male. His prison systems are full of it and his leading movie making venue, Hollywood, is packed with gay whites from all ethnic groups – Jews, Slavs, Italians, Germans and so on. It may be an unspoken requirement that you have to submit to having another man screw you up the ass in order to make it in Hollywood. And every man – black and white – has to pass this "test." Women have a "casting couch" set up by their white agents, why would there not be such a process for men as well?

Even during his "hazing" games that he plays on fellow whites as part of his fraternity system, his police hazings, the hazing initiations that he imposes when a new student enters college or high school – all have a smidgen of homosexuality to them. He likes to play with the dicks and butts of other men. This country was founded by a bunch of powder wig wearing assholes, so what can you expect? He thinks its historical, funny and cute. He pinches asses in the locker room, snaps towels on the asses of his naked teammates and, of course, is on the downlow as much as his main copycat, the black man, is. He may be a demi-god, but when all is said and done he paved the way for the homosexual orientation that today's black man now exhibits.

But the omnipotent administrator, the self-proclaimed demi-god, keeps his homosexuality on "the downlow" for the most part (maybe that's where the black man learned it).But his politics are far more power-oriented than his liking of other men. The fact is, the American white man's politics would be cartoonish if the impact of his laws and policies didn't have such a profoundly negative and discriminatory impact on localities and, indeed, the entire world.

Before even dealing with the traditional politics (Democrats, Republicans, Independent, Libertarian and the rest of those pontificating control freaks), there are several other political strategies that have been employed for centuries, politics that give form and function to the political atmosphere of today's American society.

There are the politics of Manifest Destiny and White Man's Burden, which serve as the foundation of the white supremacist system that we live in and are controlled by. The white man has always believed that the world belonged to him and him alone, from the days of the Roman Empire to the present day. He has created a "a globally accepted system" where all that is white is good, fair and universal and all that is black is evil, inferior and good. If something is "tainted" –

which means color is added – it is somehow no good. If something is "stained" – meaning that it is no longer white – then it is inferior. If someone has a "checkered past," this is a negative because the red squares are offset by the negative black ones – like a checkerboard.

And this kind of thinking permeates the literature and the popular culture from pre-school through graduate studies. This lends itself to the belief that the lack of skin color (whiteness) is the pinnacle of greatness, hence his "demi-God, blondes have more fun" status.

There are the politics of fear, from fear of population explosions to fear of black people overrunning their communities and ravaging their daughters. This is related to the previous white oriented belief system because the politics of fear are usually the politics of the fear of losing control to the "colored peoples" of the world. This has existed throughout his history. He uses his culture and system to rule through fear: scare the masses of white people with rumors of wars – racial and religious – and they will then submit to those who are making the decisions and follow suit. They will move to the suburbs, arm their families, accept racial and residential segregation, maintain the system of racial discrimination – whatever is needed to keep things "white" and keep black people down – and out.

A key component and cog of the demi-god status of the white man is his ability to dupe millions of people into accepting what he stands for although he may not stand for anything. Once stripped of all the pomp and impious ceremony, you get a chance to see many of these major power brokers for what they are: men with deep-seated feelings of inadequacy and a longing to convince the world that they are the ultimate decision makers. Two men immediately come to mind.

In an August 2014 survey, the two men in the world who were voted "most likeable" were (1) the Pope and (2) Bill Clinton. Say what???

In the case of the Pope, he's the leader of the Catholics, one of the most corrupt religious "organizations" in the history of the world, and most assuredly the most racist. It was a Catholic priest, Bartolome Las Casas, who suggested that instead of enslaving Native Americans, white folks should go to Africa and bring back a bunch of black people. The Natives knew the land too well and they were sickly because of white folks' diseases. The Africans, on the other hand, had experienced some contact with whites and weren't as likely to get sick, they were excellent farmers and apparently much stronger.

In 1857, it was Catholic Chief Justice Roger Taney who made the ruling in the Dred Scott decision that, "A black man has no rights that a white man was bound to respect." These are but two examples, but don't forget that the Catholics were among the staunchest groups resisting school desegregation back in the 1950s and 1960s. Today , because of white manipulation of history and reality, many people don't know these facts. Boys Town, rumored to be a bastion of child perverts (remember the Franklin Credit Union controversy?) is controlled by Catholics as is the entire state of Nebraska.

Then there's former President Bill Clinton (who prances around the world acting as if he is STILL the President).

Clinton, who hails from racist Arkansas, bamboozled Black people so much that Black leadership (the NAACP, for one) was going around talking about Clinton was "our first black president." Ain't that a bitch? That's some likeability for yo' ass when a white southerner is give such props from the most oppressed community in the nation. And check this out: black people were falling for this lie at the same time that Clinton was putting more cops on the street than any previous president, including Nixon! Clinton is the one who came up with these Federal minimum sentencing guidelines that ended up trapping black kids in prison for years based on some kind of "checklist." That was Clinton. And yet he's "the most likeable."

In both cases it becomes clear that the politics of these power brokers rests on the ability to get people to see what you want them to see, and to have an institutional arrangement that backs you up. In the case of the Pope, it is the Catholic church; in the case of Clinton, it is the U.S. government, more specifically the office of the presidency.

But the politics of the demi-god, the manner in which the Omnipotent Administrator keeps his power, is to also debase or do away with any prospective challenges. While there may not be many on the modern day front (except for China and India), there certainly were some back in the day. And these people, black people, were smart enough to leave behind monuments and structures that the white man was so jealous of that he tried to destroy or deface some of them. A case in point are the pyramids of Egypt and Giza.

So jealous is this white man to this present day, he is still willing to spend tens of millions of dollars attempting to show that black people (Egyptians) could NOT have built the pyramids and the other huge structures in Africa. Instead, he comes forth, led by Erik von Danikan, and writes a book called *Chariots of the Gods*:Unsolved Mysteries (1969). He's followed that up with more bullshit, including *The Ancient Alien Question* (2011), *Twilight of the Gods* (2010), *Evidence of the Gods* (2011), *Remnants of the Gods* (2013), and others. In these books it is announced that space aliens came to earth and built the pyramids.

In addition to the publications of the aforementioned books, other white "scholars" have come forth with similar claims. In fact there are movies ("Stargate," "Predators") where aliens came to Africa, became "gods," built the pyramids, and then left.

Many of the inventions that could and would have empowered black people and generated black pride were stolen by the white man in order to maintain the illusion that he is all-knowing and all-powerful. Next time you stop at a traffic light, remember that it was invented by a black man; the next time you're sweating from the heat, remember that a black man invented the air conditioner. Yes, whitey will concede the peanut-related work that George Washington Carver did – but they won't tell you that Carter was attacked by white boys when he was a kid and they cut his dick off.

This is all about revisionist history and that's why a peanut inventor is propped up and white folks feel comfortable remembering him. But since black people invented and created so much more, such a petty contribution to modern American reality is actually an insult. So again, it is not enough to glorify yourself, but there also has to be a consequent debasement of anyone who may have the potential to win over the attention of huge publics.

There are the politics of economic control, which he has succeeded in making America into a worldwide phenomenon. This is somewhat related to the previous set of politics, but it is actually the basis of most of them. As Karenga (1967) once wrote, "you cannot have political freedom without an economic base." White folks have long known this which is why they deny economic empowerment to most groups unless miniscule "donations" are doled out to those who do the bidding of the system. Anyone with a contrary view, or a perspective that is not sanctioned by the white decision maker, need not apply or if you do apply, expect to have your ideas ripped off even while the rejection letter is in the mail.

<u>Popular Culture</u>

Much of what the white man offers in the area of music is copied or outright stolen, but in addition to television, an area that he dominates is his propaganda-laden big screen movies. Through the use of super-audio of various types, 3-D and of course computer-generated imagery, he can add to the myth that he is, indeed, a deity.

For example, "In a city like New Orleans, one man embodies its spirit," says a promo for the upcoming NCIS: New Orleans program" (CBS). What? New Orleans is majority black and yet this white man (played by Scott Bakula) is the embodiment of the soul, flavor and culture of that city? Like some kind of deity, the white man projects himself as being all things to all people. In today's America he's "the greatest dancer," he can out-croon anyone, Elvis is the "king," the strongest man in the world (ala "Superman,"), the fastest man in the world (ala "Flash"), and he's irresistible, not only to all women but even to other men.

Even regular white kids can be made to look infallible. He uses his new wave cartoons to further exaggerate his power and worth to world affairs.

Touching and emotional though they may be, the image of the white man in movies is, more often than not, a gross exaggeration.

His movies can make him capable of anything: defying gravity and the laws of physics, being in more than one place at the same time, having the power to render himself invisible, traveling through time, becoming a marksman who never misses (even on his very first attempts), the inventor of everything, able to seduce any women from anywhere in the universe, becoming the fastest man on earth, or the smartest man in the world and so on. It takes place in the name of "popular culture" but it is actually a metaphor for how this megalomaniac wants people to perceive him and these behaviors and images are also the goals that he envisions for himself to make up for his minority status on a worldwide level.

Let's take a look at some examples of his movies and what they contribute to the white man status as "demi-god."

"Man of Steel"

This is white nationalism in its purest form in that the image and the message that emanates from that image is clear: white people are universal and there are other planets with whites on them. In fact, it is a primary example of the existence of the mentality and image of "an omnipotent administrator.

Jor-El, Superman's father, makes this clear when he tells the Kryptonians who will listen that he's scanned the galaxy and found a planet that will not only sustain Kryptonian life, but also has a population of people "similar to ourselves." Later in the movie Jor-El, speaking to Kal-El (Superman's real name) through a high tech archive of some kind, tells him, in preparing him, that he will be able to "fit in among the earthlings." Clearly he was talking about white folks.

It's a combination of "Romeo and Juliet" and "Hercules." Superman falls for a white woman (as did Thor) and no matter how busy he is, he finds time to "rescue" her. And this gets into another issue.

What they show is this white man who can fly, has x-ray vision, heat vision and super breath, rescuing people, keeping planes from crashing, saving giant ships that are sinking and so on. But ask yourself this: what are the bases for his choices? How does he make his selections regarding who, all over the world, is in the worst situation? You know the answer. If a hundred white folks are dying say, in Boston and ten thousand Africans are dying in Botswana, you know he's going to choose the white people in Beantown for two reasons: first, they're white and secondly, they're Americans. This is the unspoken message that I don't hear anyone discussing or addressing. Super man, who has the same skin color as the majority of the people in America (implying that the genetically recessive white man actually exists in other parts of the universe) would have to be a "race man" and as such, a racist based on his decisions.

Superman's presence could go directly against the Military-Industrial Complex. He could stop the war in the Middle East and make the Jews back off. He could straighten out Syrian civil war and deal with all those warlords in Africa. But if he did, this would threaten weapons sales and that would affect America's economy. This was an issue regarding weapons sales that was raised in "White House Down." If there are no guns, tanks, missiles, mines, grenades and rocket-to-air missiles to sell, tens of thousands of people would be out of work. There might be less war, but America would not be able to tolerate it. Superman would eventually become the enemy of Captain America *and* "G.I. Joe"!

Throughout the movie, from Jor-El's lectures, the beliefs in the baby by his mother, Lara and the on-going prompting from his "adopted father," Pa Kent (Kevin Costner) to the cheerleading claims of Ma Kent (Diane Lane), Kal-El (Superman) is told that his presence, if discovered, is going to change the world. Jor-El claims that the child will grow up to enable Earth to avoid the mistakes made by the doomed Krypton. There are references to the fact that growing up under a yellow son (Krypton's is red), he will be strong, have incredible powers and in fact, "he'll be a god." And it is here is where the racist message is most entrenched.

Since Superman represents the "American way," that means that he represents American (read: white) interests. And since, throughout this two hour and twenty-three minute movie, it appears that he has no interest in battling racism, then *that means that he has accepted it as part of the fabric of America!* There is not a single mention of the glass ceiling (gender discrimination in employment against women) although Lois Lane has to be underpaid although Perry White (played by Laurence Fishburne of all people) uses the fact that she's "under contract" to keep her from quitting. There is not a single mention of racism even though in this movie, Perry White is a black man running a white newspaper in a major city.

"Wolverine" –

Like Superman, this is another comic book hero who is indestructible – another example of "the omnipotent administrator. He is one of the X-Men, a group of mutants who are treated as if they were niggas (isolated, segregated, chased down, hunted). As s mutant, Wolverine has been operated on by some super scientists and has a body that is filled with a skeletal structure that is metal. He can spring giant claws from his fists and when injured, his wounds heal automatically.

With that out of the way it should not surprise anyone that this movie is very political and, like Superman, very ethnocentric. In this case, we find Wolverine – who is, by the way *immortal* – is in an underground holding cell during what appears to be the American bombing of Nagasaki. This was the second time a nuclear bomb was dropped on Japan (the first one having been on Hiroshima). Wolverine saves the life of one of the Japanese officers and somehow this man bonds with Wolverine, although they have not seen each other for years.

The movie is about genetic manipulation. The Japanese guard knows of Wolverine's power and knows that Wolverine doesn't want to be super any more, just wants to be a regular white boy. This is because he lost his long-time love Jean (in earlier episodes) who he had to kill because she had been turned evil by Magneto. At any rate he's a loner but this cute Asian chick is sent to fetch him so that the Japanese officer, who is dying but who is the head of a mega-sized research lab, can say his last good-byes to his "friend."

The movie is also about culture. In one scene as Wolverine and the heiress sit down to eat, he has his chop sticks stuck into some meat, standing vertically as he opts to use a fork. She gently takes them and places them on the table, letting him know that chop sticks that are standing represent antagonism of some kind. Even after that the scene continues and then he does it again. And once again this proud woman gently takes the chop sticks and sets them down. We learn that when it comes to the proper use of a Japanese sword, you use two hands, not one. And we learn that the vaunted Ninjas are known, in the early days of their formation, as "the black clan."

The Japanese guy, now head of a huge corporation, has a simple plan: since he knows Wolverine doesn't like immortality or his super powers, he (the Japanese) has a way where Wolverine's powers can be transferred to HIM, therefore enabling Wolverine to become mortal, eventually fall in love and die of old age. But Wolverine knows that his powers are not always a blessing and tells the man, "You don't want what I've got."

The plot thickens because, unbeknownst to us, the Japanese guy has willed all his finances and corporate power of Yashida Industries, to his grand daughter. The bad guys want her out of the picture and try to assassinate her. Aided by the cute Asian chick who flew him to Japan, Wolverine and the heir take off and try to hide. Along the way Wolverine's powers have been weakened because some blonde mutant female blew some kind of smoke into his lungs during a kiss.

So the Japanese guy wants the white man's genetic code and his powers – he wants eternal life. The white man with the powers simply wants to get on with his life and get as much pussy as possible. Two of the most beautiful women I've seen, who just happen to be Asian, are slobbering all over this guy, one as a self-appointed "body guard" and the other who has slept with him, inherits an empire and begs him to stay (which, of course, in line with the "lone wolf motif," he turns down).

At no time does anyone mention the fact that America was behind the dropping of that bomb. Even when Wolverine and the heiress return to Nagasaki, he references the hole that he and her grandfather dived into to escape the explosion's radiation, but America is not indicted or held responsible a single time for making the racist decision to drop a bomb on a race of people who, to this day, feel the effects of those two bombs being dropped on their two major cities. So it's selective history wrapped around a racially (genetic) driven movie.

"World War Z"

Even an omnipotent administrator can make mistakes every now and then. And when such an individual does, the whole world catches hell.

In this movie, the white man has done something wrong in the laboratory and a virus haa and spread all over the world. They claim the "source" of the disease that transforms the dead into the walking dead is elsewhere, but you know the U.S. has its hand in it. Brad goes all over the world to find a cure. You know that the Jews are involved in the script because they even went to Israel, a nation usually kept out of any movie that has to do with a pandemic because the blame for such disasters is usually blamed on brown people from the Middle East (e.g., Iran, Iraq, Afghanistan, Syria, Saudi Arabia, etc).

I'll spoil it from you: the zombies will only attack and eat you if you're healthy. Brad Pitt -- (again, the 'super man" is motif is apparent from the beginning to the end of this film) "discovers" this fact based on his personal observations. This is a theme borrowed from "Species," where black Mykelti Williamson was not approached by the sexy alien because he had sickle cell trait. In this flick Pitt notices, deduces and otherwise "solves" a problem that has escaped every scientist on earth.

And although it's only a theory, he turns out correct and saves the day. Again, he is ex-military, has medical training, and is fearless as he leaves his family to head to all parts of the world to search for the source of the virus. He even survives the crash of a jetliner! As was the case in "The Purge," and "Man of Steel," the "super white man" risks his own life to save the world. In this particular movie, Pitt injects himself with a virus and then, to test it on the spot, walks down a hallway filled with maniacal and hungry zombies.

At any rate the solution is to infect everybody with some kind of virus which will render that person invisible as far as the zombies are concern. "Then we can fight and defeat them," Brad says at one point. Let me get this straight: infect yourself with something that will make you sick and possibly kill you so that you won't get killed by a zombie.

"The Purge"

Just when you thought that themes about chasing down black people were gone with "Native Son," "Big Boy Goes Home," and the "The Defiant Ones", here we go with "The Purge." The overall theme is that this is the new America of the future, and under the new rules, crime becomes legal for one day out of the year. You have to do what you need to do to protect yourself, your family and your property from 9pm until 7 in the morning. The hero, Ethan Hawke, sells home security systems and is making a killing (no pun intended).

Now here's where the racism comes in. As the purge night begins, it seems that all should be alright. Hawke, his wife and two kids have a hi-tech home with steel shields sliding down over the windows, and so on. As they're chilling upstairs, the teenage boy hears a knocking on the door. It's a black man seeking refuge, asking to be let in because some people are after him and trying to kill him. He's bloody and desperate and the white kid lets him in. The parents come downstairs and the brutha witnesses Hawke shoot down the boyfriend of the teenage girl who tried to shoot Hawke (it's never explained why). Hawke kills him but this gives the brutha time to flee to another part of the house and hide from these crazy peckerwoods.

But wait! There are even crazier ones outside, shades of "Clockwork Orange." The leader tells Hawke who is peering out of the peephole that "we're like you. We're highly educated and have good jobs." He says everything except "hand over the nigger." Here is the fact that is implied: the purge is about giving "Americans" a chance to vent their anger and frustration once a year and in doing so, this had led to a 1% unemployment rate and a peaceful way of life.

But on purge night, they know good and well that it is the black and the poor who are going to be preying on each other because they cannot afford those security systems, they live in areas where there is great need and, since crime is legal, they can prey on each other. At one point someone says, "sooner or later the purge will enable us to get rid of all of 'them.'" They never say "blacks," but you know what they mean.

Where is the theme of the "omnipotent administrator" in the film, "The Purge"? Well just think about it: (1) the white man has found a way to get leadership to vote for a "day of violence" as a cure for America's internal problems; (2) the white man has gotten the American public to accept this idea and, as a result, crime has gone down and unemployment is almost non-existent; (3) if we are to believe this movie, a white family living in a segregated, gated, upper-class community and has one child (the boy) who has enough compassion to open up the door for a bleeding and sweating black man (super-morals?); (4) Ethan Hawke in defense of his "house and family" blows away and otherwise kills at least seven bad guys (and girls) before finally making the supreme sacrifice (the same way Superman supposedly does when he risks his life to fight other super-people in defense of the American way).

The concept of a purge is more than what this popular culture movie projects to the American public. A "purge" is defined in several ways that are most relevant to the theme of this paper and to the concept of an "omnipotent administrator. The relevant definitions are, as follows: "To clear (a container or space, for example) of something unclean or unwanted; To remove or eliminate unwanted physical matter: to rid (a person or thing) of something unwanted; To remove or eliminate (an unwanted element): To rid (a nation or political party, for example) of people considered undesirable; To get rid of (people considered undesirable)." They key here is that purging involves getting rid of something that is deemed unwanted and undesirable.

Who do you think this country has been trying to "purge" from its population rolls in recent years? Latinos. And who has this country waged a purge since slavery was abolished? Black people. The omnipotent administrator realizes that all the shoes have been shined and all the cotton has been picked. So he starts locking up black people, most of them unemployed. The Latinos are willing to do the menial work but because they are people of color, the white supremacist system doesn't have too much tolerance for them, either.

"White House Down"
Just because you have a black President (as is the case in this movie) doesn't mean that shit is going to change, as I tried to tell my brothers and sisters when Barack got elected. The president of the United States is not the "omnipotent administrator" – he follows orders from, among others, the Tri-lateral Commission, the Skulls, the Illuminati and a host of secret societies that are the ones truly in control of this country (and the world, for that matter). This movie lends credence to my statements. What do we find? We find that the military is behind the attack on the White House because the President (Jamie Foxx) is opposed to war and doesn't want any more military contracts – he wants peace in the Middle East.

Enter a "superman" who is a former military man who served in Iraq and is now vying to join the Secret Service. In this movie even though outmanned and out-gunned, he performs one "super feat" after another. He defeats trained military personnel (mercenaries) , all in the name of saving his little girl, who is presented as being "super" in her own right. In fact, she is the real hero of the movie: she is the one who takes pictures of the bad guys who have infiltrated the white house and then emails it to officials; she is the one who stands up to the leader of the bad guys by staring down a gun, not once but twice. She is the one who takes the flag at the end of the movie and signals an air strike force not to "blow up" the White House saying, in essence, my daddy has everything under control.

This pisses off the military decision makers and their "in-house collaborators" who enable military trained personnel to infiltrate the White House, blow up Air Force One (with people on board), gain access to missile systems and everything else. Jamie makes the point that America is not for sale and that the military is doing this so that they can continue making money. And this is an example of art imitating life.

But what is the overriding message? A trainee who didn't pass muster when he trained for the Secret Service and a United States president can out-think, out-muscle, out-perform and outlast a squad of trained mercenaries. White House Down" hints that white America will think that the destruction of the White House is caused by "Al Qaeda" (brown people) but it's really white dudes. Even though the mercenaries are white, don't forget that they are doing all this to capitalize on America's racist belief that "terrorists" (read: middle eastern brown men) are going to destroy their way of life, starting with taking over the White House.

"The Lone Ranger"

This story is, in my view, the western frontier version of "Superman." One might say that the theme of an "omnipotent administrator" is implied when you have this white man, on a white horse, hiding behind a mask and a white hat, riding around and kicking anybody who is a threat to the system. All this is, of course, done in the name of "fighting for justice." But to paraphrase Richard Pryor, when white folks talk about "justice" they are talking about themselves – "just us."

After all, the Lone Ranger existed because he was riding with seven other rangers and got cut down in an ambush. He was the "lone" survivor and was rescued by a Native American who he named Tonto. Tonto is a Pottowotomie Indian word that means "wild one." Some people say it means, "fool." Tonto's horse in the original series was named Scout, but before that, do you know what he was named? White Fella. Do you think this is an accident, since the Lone Ranger's horse is called "Silver"?

Like Superman, at least in this movie, this white man was deemed to be a "spirit walker" who could not be killed. At one point when Tonto is fighting a bad guy atop a train moving at top speed, the Lone Ranger, riding Silver while atop another train moving parallel to the first train, fires a shot that hits a club out of a bad guy's hand. Before shooting he says to himself, "I'm a spirit walker – I can't miss." So he had bullshitted himself to believe that he was omniscient in the same way that future generations would view Superman and the way the American military views itself.

The historical truths uncovered in this movie did assuage some of the racism of it. Although a Comanche tribe is wiped out (twice), at least it showed brave warriors going forth and taking on the cavalry and the train company. The movie showed the lying ways of the white man, the "official" way that the train company ("progress") broke treaties, the Chinese working in relative anonymity on the railroads (especially in the tunnels), and a few token blacks shown in with no real relevance to the movie (as usual).

The rest of the movie is wrapped in jokes, quips, obscure bullshit and violence. In my view it is racist to take a white man, put him on a white horse and in a white hat, and have him ride with a Native American who, in every way, was superior. The native brutha knew the country better, he was smarter, he was more spiritual (not "Christian," but spiritual), he was stronger and he was rougher all around.

And yet in the white man's mind (using the omnipotent administrator motif), this guy from back east, educated in law and very green, is going to come out west, ride with his brother (who was a Texas ranger), who had no gun training but "used to box for the law school," can come to the wild west, get shot down, rise up, get shot with an arrow, rise up, develop a plan to take down a giant railroad organization, know how to use a lasso, ride a powerful horse, use that horse to jump from a parallel hillside to land atop a moving train, and so on. Only a white audience would eat this shit up.

"Pacific Rim" –

Pacific Rim is "Superman" in a hi-tech, gigantic suit, built by the white man so that he can fight the "monsters' on equal terms. It's another example of the mentality of "the ominipotent administrator." It's a rip off of "Transformers" for the most part, and it's an extension of the same racism even though a black man (Idris Alba) is the "leader" of this group of military tech heroes whose job it is to fight and fend off giant sea creatures who are attacking the earth in droves.

At one point the nerdy scientist (a Jew of course) makes the statement that "numbers never lie" and adds, "numbers are the closest thing we have to touching the hand of God." Say what? The white man can think and lock minds with the creatures and defeat the creature in his own turf – miles underwater in what is called "the breach" but comes awfully close to the way that the white Christian would define "hell." Of course the white invented robot gear that is designed can withstand anything, and this leads me to an important point about a message aimed at the Millennials.

A point that many people may not make much of is when these people offer a theory of who these creatures are. Guess what they come up with? The creatures who are attacking the world now are the descendants of the dinosaurs. You see, some intelligent life is controlling all these monsters. So millions of years ago they sent the dinosaurs out and they couldn't survive because of the environment, so they died off. The smart creatures behind all this (we hardly see them until the end) then wait and send out a new batch, having improved on the "mistake" that they made in the dinosaur age. And even among this new, giant breed, they have the capacity to adapt so the first group comes up and gets backed up: a second wave comes up and has reached level 3 and then come the super giant creatures who are an upgrade on all of the previous ones. They can adapt , they can think and they can anticipate.

Because so many of these young people watch video games and play them, and because these games are mega-violent, the white movie producers know that violence has to be a heavy theme. Never before in film history, including war movies, has there been so much heavy background sound: bombs, bullets, loud thunderous crashes and so on. More mental manipulation and programming by the self-proclaimed demi-god.

Linked to that sound that permeates the theater is an incredible amount of property destruction throught the movie. It was depicted heavily in Superman, who took an asswhipping all through the film, which led to the destruction of an entire city (Metropolis) in the process. In his quest to "defend" Metropolis, he basically tore it up: buildings, railroad cars, corporate towers, huge chunks of asphalt and concrete ripped out of the earth. The same thing in "White House Down:" (tearing up the White House and the surrounding area, blowing planes out of the sky), "Transformers," "The Avengers" (utterly destroying an American city as they fought to "defend it"), and numerous others. There seems to be a competition among these action movie makers to see which one can fuck up the most shit.

Another dimension is that the white man's racism is aimed at the Millennials in an attempt to show them that the scope of white influence is no longer limited to a particular city, state or the nation. Now they have gone "international" with their racist depictions of white supremacy. As stated, "World War Z" features countries all over the world including Israel. "Fast and Furious 6" begins in Brazil and then goes all over the world battling the bad guys. More evidence of the "omnipotent administrator" mentality.

The Christians talk about God being omnipotent (all powerful), omniscient, and all knowing. If you see these movies, even the ones that are pawned off as comedies, these white folks are seen as being universally accepted everywhere they go, always coming out on top, able to venture anywhere and money is never an issue. They are always being accepted and sought after all over the world – as long as those people work FOR them and do their bidding. The Omnipotent Administrator wins again.

"R.I.P.D." –

The mythical belief that there are white people in the place called "Heaven" is one of the biggest dupes of all time. We've seen the Norse "gods (Odin, Thor, Loki), the Roman gods (Jupiter, Venus, Apollo) and even the Greek gods (Zeus,

Poseidon, Hades, Apollo, etc.). The Christians have a giant white man in outer space (or so go the depictions of him) and a place called "Heaven" where, if you're good little boy or girl, you'll go. This is where RIPD picks up: the bullshit belief in an "afterlife."

That's right. RIPD stands for Rest In Peace Department, a giant police department in the sky, a place for "the best lawmen who lived and died." Your job is to bring back the folks that died but won't stay dead, back to that place to be arrested and judged. Everybody up there is, of course white as far as I could see, and they get super powers including new identities and they go back to Earth to handle their business. This puts yet another twist on the concept of an "omnipotent administrator."

This movie ought to have these moralizing Christians outraged. But they can't say anything because the Jews that sanction these movies might also get angry. And you can believe that Jews are involved in all of this bullshit that I'm talking about: they are the writers, the casting directors, the distributors, the executive producers and the people behind the cameras. They approve all this shit, lend the money to make the movies and then distribute these "white supremacist"-themed films all over the world. No one says anything about the ethnicity of the people making this shit because for some reason, they're afraid. Just knowing that they're white people seems to be good enough.

"The Conjuring" –

The concept of white supremacy is what produces such images and characters as "Superman" (all powerful), Aquaman (controller of the seas), Wonder Woman (an amazon with super powers), Batman (super smart and virile), Thor (the Norse "god of thunder" that exists in their mythology that came to comic books and is now a hit on film), the Hulk (white man is a genius but creates a laser/radiation beam that puts color in his skin and when he turns green, he goes berserk), The Flash (super speed), Daredevil (blind man with super acrobatic powers, is an attorney by day), Spiderman (punk kid gets bitten by a Spider and gets super powers, speed and fights crime for free), and so many more. These are all derivatives and variations of the "omnipotent administration" theme.

But in the white supremacy culture, it is equally important to show that just "regular white folks" can also be masters of their domain and of those around them. This is where "The Conjuring" comes in. People want us to believe that in November of 1971, this shit really happened. That is bullshit, plain and simple. A family moves into a house that is "haunted" as in so many other movies ("Poltergeist," Trick R Treat, "Silent Hill," "Paranormal Activity," "Hostel," "1408," "House on Haunted Hill," "Amityville Horror," "The Haunting," "Dream House" etc.). In this particular film, the demons must be "exorcised" from the home and that is where we find the link between white supremacy and the white view of their religious beliefs. As I've written elsewhere, the white man sees religion and the concept of "god" as nothing less than an extension of his own power, hence, the concept of "omnipotent administrator."

In this movie the Catholic church gets all this credit for being able to "exorcise" demons, not only from individuals, but also from houses. It is no longer enough to "exorcise" the devil from human beings; now we have a residential structure and, as the pastor points out, "This house needs an exorcism." There are criteria for you to qualify to have an exorcism performed, we learn. You have to be a member of the (Catholic) church, the kids involved (one was being possessed by a demon) have to have been baptized and third, you have to have approval from the Vatican. What?

This movie didn't hold true to that because the guy that performed the exorcism for the family that was having the problems had kids that weren't baptized (at one point he says we were eventually going to get around to it) and they DIDN'T get the permission from the Vatican, although at movie's end the writers made it a point to throw in a final scene where the couple that performed the exorcism "finally got the call from the Vatican."

But these whites had already solved the problem, defeated the devil, and all is well.

This whole idea of ghost hunters, haunted artifacts and these apparitions is a recurring themes in these movies (as in the case of "This Is The End"). All of this pays into the white man's view of himself and the pervasiveness of his power. And of course, there is the flip side: since all religious, saintly, holy and spiritual power equates to white power, then expect references to evil (as in this movie) to be regarded as "a DARK spirit." Or how about this line: "I've been seeing the DARK entity that haunts your family – it's feeding off you."

According to this white supremacy-based bullshit, there are three phases to someone being taken over by the evil. These stages are, first of all "infestation," where a bunch of evil spirits congregate in a body and, as in this case, an actual house. Second is "oppression," and that's where they start playing pranks on you, messing with lights, slamming doors and, in short, scaring the living shit out of you. Third is "possession," and that's where the evil spirit takes control and sees you and anyone else as an invader or outsider.

This system has followed this formula and has taken over the minds of the American public. The "omnipotent administrator" has "transformed the sex roles of the public and most people don't seem to give a damn.

"Elysium"

This movie is about "white flight" at the scientific and futuristic level. If you weren't convinced that the majority of this country is going to be Latino in a few years, this movie, which takes place in 2154 will surely convince you. It's an incredible movie, a direct rip off of race relations in this country, stripped from the annals of white interpretation, dipped into a batter of intergalactic bullshit, and the put on the screen so that viewers, especially the Millennials, will think that "man, this couldn't happen" when, in reality, it's already happening right in the face of these young idiots.

This is a story about Trey and Max, a cute Latina and a white dude who grew up together in the slums, or that is, what is left of Earth. Max has adapted as they grew up and went their separate ways. Trey was smart and left to become a nurse while he was a hustler, car thief and thug who ends up doing blue collar assembly line grunt work in some hi-tech factor (don't forget this is the 22nd century). They pledge themselves to each other with tattoos, but it's not much more than that. In reality, Max would be a black man from the South in the 1940s working in the most hazardous areas of any plant or factory. But all they have to do is steal this reality, flip it, make the hard working guy a white boy, and these Millennials – who know about as much about history as a wino knows about building a laser gun – won't know the difference.

While working for corporate giant Armadyne, Max's boss forces him to un-jam a machine and Max gets caught in it and is exposed to a fatal dose of radiation (shades of Yaphet Kotto in "Blue Collar," where he was intentionally locked in a paint room at a car factor and was killed). Of course the boss who assigned Max to "fix it" knew it was hazardous and as Max is carried out of the radiation filled chamber, the boss disappears. This is the way they treated black men during the 1940s in the foundries in Detroit when it would get so hot their work boots would literally melt.

At any rate, Max doesn't die, but is told by the doctors that he has only five days to live. While he's at the hospital he runs across Trey, who has returned and is working as a nurse. They begin to rekindle what they once had.

As both "We're the Miller" and "2 Guns" made clear, Latinos are the order of the day. "Elysium is no exception. The part of the world they are in, America, is not predominantly Latino and I didn't see three blacks together throughout the entire movie. At any rate, Frey's young daughter has a physical disability. Now, we've established the relationship, we have to talk about context.

"Elysium," is perhaps one of the goals of the omnipotent administrator in real life: more segregation, this time based on class, not just race. They get all the good stuff – space, land, good health care, clean air, luxury – and the vast majority of people don't get shit. And then they ship it away from Earth up to this planet that they have named Elysium, and leave Earth to wither away like the last leaves of a painfully prolonged autumn. Is this not the way it was during "white flight" in the 1960s when blacks move to the city and white folks immediately packed up, left and created "the suburbs"?

That is what "Elysium" originally was. It was a place of ideal happiness that you went to after you died – akin to the "Heaven" that these Christians believe in so deeply. But take notice of this: just like in the title and theme of the television show "Happy Days," please not that the concept of ultimate happiness on Elysium is a planet with what? No niggas around!

This movie featured Latinos because that is the trick that is being used on the Millenials. Just as "World War Z" had a global, somewhat "third world" flavor, and "2 Guns" had a Mexican flavor, "Wolverine" had a definitive Asian flavor, and "Lone Ranger" was Native American, so it is with "Elysium" and its thrust toward Latinos from top to bottom: love interest, bad guys, corporate brains and so on. The omnipotent administrator is more committed to his "whiteness" than he is to any "ism," and that's why he is more than happy to toss his white woman to the "colored" wolves and let her assume the role of *direct* oppressor, while he wallows in his own man-made "Elysium" and assumes the role of demi-god.

This "multicultural cast" dupes young people into thinking that everybody's the same, while the racist message of these white boys coming out as winners in every single scenario, is ingrained in their minds and as such, the myth of white supremacy, and the rule of the omnipotent administrator, are maintained and perpetuated.

Sure, it's a movie NOW, but the theme is so typical of the white boy: he creates another world, basically a giant satellite revolving around polluted earth, where only the wealth can live. In other words, for whites only.

Wasn't that the same way it was during the days of legal segregation and isn't that the way it still is with all these "gated communities" and "upscale habitats"? Isn't that the way it is today as the white families surround themselves in gated communities (ala "The Purge") and live out in areas where their driveways are wider than some of the main thoroughfares in the inner city? And as it is in real life, Elysium is the place where there is fresh air (ala the suburbs) and where you can get top notch medical care, including cures for all diseases.

Meanwhile, earthlings inhale polluted air, live in the midst of squalor and suffer from high population density in high crime. In other words, a re-creation of the ghetto and *el barrio*.

"Star Trek: Into Darkness"

The nation has made octillions of dollars promoting that "white is good and black is bad" bullshit; it's a part of white culture. So when you see the word "darkness," you know that something fucked up is about to take place, something negative and evil. That is the on-going imagery being promoted and promulgated by the omnipotent administrator.

On the other hand, "Star Trek" is a multi-billion dollar enterprise, starting off with the 1960s television show that starred William Shatner and Leonard Nimoy. Following that five year stint, a few years later came the movies, reprising both the roles of Shatner (Captain James T. Kirk) and Nimoy (Science Officer Spock). After about five or six of these mediocre movies, the decision makers rested a while and then, in the name of the Millennials who they wanted to appeal to, they came back strong with a "Star Trek" crew that was younger, more hip and, at least when it came to Kirk, more daring and deviant.

But these assholes were colonizers. Although the "prime directive" made it clear that they were not to interfere or fuck with alien cultures, but only to "seek out new life and new civilizations and boldly go where no man has gone before," they violated that shit every week. In this particular movie, a theme that moviegoers can relate to: terrorism. This time, it's on an intergalactic scale. The bad guy is pissed off at the Federation and decides to destroy Earth as an act of payback.

Fast forward to 2013 and a review by a critic by the name of Matt Zoller Seitz. And he makes a similar observation to those I made many years ago in my reviews of the original "Star Trek." Now at the beginning of the movie the crew is on some jungle-like planet and they're running for their lives and Spock, every curious, gets left behind even as the others are "beamed on board" to a ship (the Enterprise) that had no business even being seen, lest the natives see it and the sight of such futurism alter their thinking and, by extension, their culture. Here is what Seitz astutely pieces together:

> The correct thing to do is leave Mr. Spock behind, because going back to rescue him would violate the Federation's Prime Directive against messing with the natural development of primate cultures. It's in this opening sequence, for better or worse, that the movie establishes a vexing narrative pattern: The characters have urgently necessary arguments about the morally, ethically, and procedurally correct thing to do in a crisis, then one character (usually Kirk) makes a unilateral, straight-from-the-gut decision that worsens everything; and yet somehow at the end he's rewarded, or at least not seriously punished.

I cite this because it shows that what I have charged all these years has always been true: Kirk can do no wrong, Kirk is all-powerful, Kirk can fuck whomever he wants and say what he pleases. In a word, Kirk is GOD, a veritable omnipotent administrator in human form and white skin. That is how he was treated episode after episode back in the days of the televised version. His role doesn't make a lick of fuckin' sense: he's the Captain in yet on all of the television versions and the movies, he's taking his ass down to some planet to risk his life (instead of delegating those roles to flunkies lower on the pay scale). Not only that, but in most cases he usually drags his top ranking officers with him (among them Scotty, Chekov, Spock and of course, Sulu). All of them racial and ethnic stereotypes.

At any rate, this fits right into the brainwashing that is focused on the brainwashing of the American populace. At a time when young people of all racial backgrounds are dancing, singing, playing X-box and fucking up together, it is imperative that racial division be maintained and perpetuated. This is another role of the movies: to show that no matter how much racial progress there has been in real life, there is no doubt that the "fantasy" of everyone has to be that the white man can do whatever he wants and, as was declared in the 1857 case of *Scott v. Sanford*, "a black man has no rights that the white man is bound to respect." Just look at how they're treating Barack Obama, and he's the President of the United States!!

It's like it is in real life: the white man drinks and cavorts, gets into fights and somehow gets bailed out of it. The black man (Spock is pretty much a "nigga" as far as his treatment), though superior, spends most of his time debating with his inferiors while watching them (whites) do as they please, totally devoid of the "logic" that he claims to believe in. Of course, as the white man has done with black spirituality, he disregards that logic unless he can use it for his own ends, and in fact, though this is only the second movie of this particular franchise, it is clear that Spock is becoming assimilated.

Not only is Spock regularly claiming to be "half-human" (like the mulattoes boast of being "half white" when it suits them), he's also in love with a black woman, Uhura, played by Zoe Saldana (some boney black bitch, half Puerto Rican and half Dominican), whose real name is Zoe Yadira Saldana Nazario. She's brash and speaks numerous languages and is madly in love with Spock. The unspoken message is that she was too black for the white boys, so they gave her to this half-human asshole who only fucks a couple of times a year.

Khan is back with an improved version, a super powered white man who kicks star fleet in the ass. But much of what is done is as illogical as the behavior of the Star Trek crew claiming to about "seeking out new life and new civilizations" but not mentioning the fact that they usually find a way to fuck it up. Khan is better than these white boys at everything. When they first find him he's on another planet kicking the shit out of Klingons. Not one or two, but about two dozen of them. He goes up against their weapons, he humiliates them in hand-to-hand combat, and then even as this same Klingon crew has Star Fleet (Kirk, Spock, Uhuru) pinned down with their guns, Khan makes short work of them, therefore saving their lives.

After watching him beat the shit out of the Klingons, Kirk has the nerve to pull a gun on him and "arrest" him. That, right then and there, should have told them it was a trap and that Khan just wanted to get aboard that ship. But no, that would be too much like right.

Khan's plan is working. Once board the Enterprise, he watches as they get into scrapes and eventually need his help. Even after nearly vanquishing the crew, it is Khan's super-rich blood that is needed to save Kirk, who gets trapped in a radiation chamber the same way that Spoke did way back in the old movie "Star Trek." Spock has to chase down this super human and fight him in order to get the blood that is needed to save his buddy Kirk. Like a true flunky: "what's wrong boss, *we* sick?"

They tear up an entire city and nearly obliterate the Enterprise. They are able to get rid of Khan by shipping him off and then they stand among the rubble and claim victory. That is the same thing that these white people are going to be doing – standing amidst rubble – when these people around the world come here for "payback" for all those centuries of abuse that America heaped upon them. When that day comes, the concept of "into darkness" will come to mean the majority of white folks falling prey into the "darkness" of the skin color of the majority of the world's peoples.

Meanwhile, the omnipotent administrator will escape the fray, as he did in movies like "Elysium," "2012, "Blade Runner" and so many others.

The Omnipotent Administrator is the white man as a demi-god. He continues to rule the behaviors of everyone, sets the standards, disseminates the images, the rules and regulations that all are to obey. He is akin to the leader of the Phantom Zone prisoners in "Superman," who demanded to the president of the United States, "Kneel before Zod!" Even now CBS is preparing to air a televised version of the movie, "Limitless," about a drug created by the white man that can make the person who takes it the smartest person in the world. If that's not a "God complex," then I don't know what is.

Keep in mind that the demi-god sets the rules and policies that he imposed on everyone else. He defines what is acceptable, normal and beautiful but does so always with a tendency toward how much control each of these policies or rules can contribute to his domination of the world. He has long designed high heeled shoes for women (making it almost impossible for them to walk or run), and is gradually shortening the skirts of young girls; he has tightened up the arrests of black and brown men, thereby confusing their sexual views of women once they are released into and upon the real world; he claims to be anti-street drug but releases tons of prescription and over the counter drugs on the world, drugs that don't cure anything, but keep the population in a dazed state and dependent upon these drugs on a lifelong basis.

The demi-god still prefers the blonde, but this time around he is using her to further divide the races. So successful is his media machine he has lovely brown and dark skinned women dying their hair platinum blonde, honey blonde, and various shades. He has them in locker rooms of athletes, serving as anchors on major news shows, and even working to infiltrate the board room and military. He has continued to sew confusion and sex role change, as I have described in this book, ensures his dominance for decades to come.

So rockstrong is his rule that even if dark skinned people are elected to high office, they will only do so because they have *his* mentality and outlook on life (and death): they share his values, his corrupt mindset and his long-term goals for domination. He will use whatever it takes – law, health care, politics, education, popular culture, labor and other institutional arrangements – to make sure that he remains the standard. Even his opponents will use him as a reference point as they scrounge and scrape for jobs, civil rights, recognition, inclusion, community engagement and so on.

When people in this country go to church, they are going to pay homage to the white man, the demi-god. Oh sure, they claim "God has no race" but they say this from the confines of a segregated suburb, gated communities, the ghetto or the barrio. They say that God is not a man, but that's what the term that the Bible is bespeckled with. You see people who are happy or in pain about something and out of their distended mouths comes, "Oh my god!" They say this while staring at or referring to white judges, white cops, corporations, and money. While Christians claim that their God has everything, they build these mega-churches and plop down money into the collection plate as their Bible requires (known as "tithing"). Even when their ministers screw up, they are immediately forgiven because they were "chosen by God."

For instance, in August Kim Davis, this fat white bitch in Ashland, Kentucky (a clerk in the county offices) denied two gay men a marriage license – a clear violation of Federal and state law. The media was in full effect when one of the men asked her, "on whose authority do you deny us a license?" This woman said, "On God's authority." So it should be clear that in her view, God is the white man because as we know, God doesn't "talk" to these human assholes – they just lie and claim that it does. And as the woMAN, she takes an aggressive stand and doesn't give a shit about what anybody thinks. After all, she's a supporter of white supremacy, too!

The only "god" these fake ass people know is the white man. The Supreme Being is expected to exist "on faith" and through being a "believer." The white demi-god is changing the face of the earth with pollution and has killed millions of people in the name of being "the good guys" (his words). He has divided the races and has people on their knees praying to him every Sunday. He attacks other religious beliefs (which are bullshit in and of themselves) if they dare "complete" with his blue-eyed, blond haired Jesus figure.

CHAPTER 5:
The Gay Male as the "New Nigga"

When I say "nigga" in this context I am mostly talking about treatment and social action. The concept of "nigga" is one that was imposed on black people to affirm, maintain and perpetuate their "less than human" status in the eyes of white folks. The word "fag" was aimed at doing the same thing for homosexuals,, but their esteem was too high and the history was too short. Back when I was a young but we called them "sissies" but again, their collective ability to "fit in" enabled them to have a shield that black people – the original "niggas" – did not have.

You hear these gay people talking about, "calling us fags is like calling a back person a nigga." No it's not. They (gays) either CHOOSE to be a fags or they're born that way but we ain't got no choice but to be niggas in the eyes of the white man (the judgmental demi-god). Not only that, but if white women are racist and white men are racist and the white elderly are racist, then why would the white homosexual not also be racist? So despite the fact that he faces ridicule from society, no matter how bad things get, he (the gay) can always look down at Black folk.

And they keep on making the comparison between black people and their own cause. David Ermold, who was denied a marriage license by the Kentucky clerk, was pissed and made a big deal of it. He asked her, on national television, if she would "deny a license to an interracial couple"? By the way, where was he and those of his ilk when interracial marriage was illegal (prior to 1970)? So if they think they're being treated like "niggas," then they are welcome because now they can be the "new niggas" and, through rallies, demonstrations and protests, fight for the rights that black people had to fight for.

The fact of the matter is that gay folk have finally started coming out of the closet and no longer is ashamed of what he or she is. Black people went through this phase of shame, and light skinned ones felt they were better than darker ones and those that were extremely light tried to "pass" – pretending to be white so they could be accepted.

Secondly, like niggas, gays are not only coming out of the closet, but are making demands to be treated fairly. In June of 2015, same-sex marriages finally became the law of the land. Gay people are continuing to confront the system in a number of ways, usually through marches and the courts. As usual, black people lead the way via the Civil Rights and Black Power Movements and others (in this case the LGBT community), after we bleed and die, fight in the streets and break down the door, come strolling in as if they were the pioneers.

Third, like niggas, most gay men and women try to stay in shape. This is what we used to do back in the day: pickup games on weekends, street races from telephone pole to telephone poll, flag football any time of the year. But then these peckerwoods loaded up American homes with video games and now our kids are fat, slow thinking, illiterate slobs who can't do anything unless they have an I-phone in their hands.

Fourth, like niggas, the gay male in particular, likes to dress and is as conscious about coordinating his clothes as he is about keeping his body in shape. The Black man used to do this and to an extent, he still does. Today the black man acts more gay than the gay does. "The problem is that this conspicuous consumption is far above our means and we often have to delve into the underground economy in order to keep those clothes, shoes and jewelry fresh. Like bitches, Black men are especially guilty of this, but the Black woman is the same way, especially with those gaudy wigs and hats and those spiked heels.

Fifth, just as the Bible was used to degrade and define black people as being the cursed descendants of Ham, the gay is also rebuked by the Bible with the passage that "man shall not lay with man." But despite this, the gays continue to contribute huge sums of money to these religious pimps and knowing that gays are upwardly mobile and have jobs, the church allows them in as long as they put money in the collection plate.

Black preachers will accept anybody as long as they pay; black gays permeate the African-American church and the same black people who put down homosexuality are the same ones who knowingly sit next to black homosexuals in church. In fact, many of the hallelujah hucksters who serve as the pastors, bishops and deacons of these churches are closet homosexuals. Therefore, the selective use of Bible passages is clear: exceptions are made for those who put great deals of money into the collection plate as well as those who pay their tithes (one-tenth of what they've earned).

The gay male has been chastised, humiliated, attacked, killed and ridiculed for centuries. Unlike the black man who could not hide his skin color and who underwent much more torture and travail, the gay male hid his gayness, married women, pretended to be a playa and was able to slip under society's radar.

Mimicking the civil rights movement as all whites have done (and benefitted from), gays have decided to "come out of the closet" that they have hidden in all these years. As the black male becomes more gay and inconsequential as a male, the gay is now coming forward in civil rights, in articulating his role and in romancing other men. It is now almost acceptable and, like the appearances of "Amos n' Andy," Stepin Fetchit and other "negroes on the silver screen and television, so now it is with the gay. But for the most part he is not ridiculed. Even those who oppose seeing gays on television or the silver screen are thwarted as these gays are usually surrounded by appealing white women to help to circumvent or deflect some of the ridicule.

In today's world, the gay male has assumed many of the social roles that were once held, rightfully and stereotypically, by the black male. In the world of fashion they promenade down the runway and pose on the covers of magazines as the "metro male." This is nothing but a code name for gay: someone who keeps his body in shape (to better take it up the ass), dresses and speaks well. This is why increasing numbers of women are dating and marrying them. To these women if you can't use the hips, use the lips. They want the sperm for reproduction, not the actual act of sex. They assist these men in hiding their sexual identities and all is well. White women AND black women are engaging in this behavior. The people who know or suspect keep quiet, and all is well. But that doesn't make him any less of a "nigga."

As the "new nigga," the gay is going to learn what happens in a society where you dress better, are much hipper and better groomed that the majority population males who may be demi-gods, but history shows that they are as slouchy as hell. But then again, they can afford to be because they have the benefit of white privilege, meaning they don't even have to have much merit, because white skin usually does the trick every time. As a result, the demi-gods and their race relatives reign supreme.

<u>CLOSING REMARKS</u>

Transformers every one. No, not those robots from another world who can shape shift into cars and trucks as you've seen on the cartoon and the big screen. I'm talking about human being and the changing sex roles which, in turn, changes the dating dynamic and the family dynamic. America is fucked up and confused, but these new sex roles and identities are where a society that is morally bankrupt eventually ends up.

There will be those who say, "No system, no institution, no group of individuals ever would or could transform so drastically or dramatically." Don't get me wrong: this transformation has been taking place over a period of about two centuries, ever since these white people – scum rejected by their English superiors – came over here and laid the groundwork for the morally loose society that you see today. Murder, deception and greed was the name of the game they played.

All along the message seemed to be "anything goes," and even their laws were biased, groups were segregated, human beings were lynched while these white folks posed and smiled for the camera, women were burned at the stake when suspected of being "witches." Self-deception about what this country was, is and will become continues to reign supreme.

I'm just sharing a theory – don't hate the playa, hate the game! After all, I have provided evidence, motive, method and opportunity to back up what I have observed and studied. My theory explains, to a large extent, some of the bullshit taking place in this country's human relationships. If we accept the transformation paradigm, then we can better understand the spate of black-on –black crime, the sky high divorce rates, children out of control, pacification of humans with more technology than they can handle, and why the world no longer respects us. What appears in movies, on television and in much of the news are all smokescreens and mirrors to keep us from collectively seeing how fucked up we are as a nation.

For instance, white movie producers and the like spent $3 million to build a movie set for the movie, "The League of Distinguished Gentlemen." After the movie was over, they tore the set down. Even some of the actors, including Sean Connery, said that they should have left it up and used it as a building for parties or raves (had the set been constructed in the United States instead of England, it would have cost closer to ten million). My point here is to show you that in order to promote a fantasy, this is the length that people with wealth and wherewithal will go through. *If that is the case, imagine what they will do, plan for and implement in the real world when they believe that their very racial history and humanity is at stake.*

And what is at stake? Everybody's going to eventually pay dues for all this shit, but my central concern is, of course, Black folks. First of all, it is a matter of simple genetics: eliminate the black woman and any black people born hereafter will have non-black mothers. Why is this important? For future "training," of course. Remember: the hand that rocks the cradle rules the throne, but is also the hand that directs the children. The less black and conscious the child is, the more confused he or she is when they ask "why do I have two mommies (or daddies)? The more confused the sister-dyke, the more power mad the white female who now wants to take charge, the more effeminate the black man becomes and the more power mad the white demi-god is, the more unstable the nation is going to be.

When it comes to black male-female relationships, one has to consider the relationship of black people in regard to the white power structure. In regard to that relationship, little has changed. If this is the case, and I say that it is, then when it comes to black male-female relationships and the question of family stability, it is understandable that there would be frustration and, as a result, abuse. Robert Hill (1993) concluded that, "black women experience disproportionate levels of mental and physical abuse from black men because of the more frequent institutional barriers and frustrations experienced by black men relative to white men" (p. 45).

But it's the entire society for the most part, that is fucked up and being impacted by these "transformations." For the first time ever it was announced in N ovember of 2015, that a boy was featured in a Barbie commercial. That's right: playing with dolls and looking like little bitches. And on the same day, actor Charlie Sheen came forward and admitted that he had contracted AIDS and was being extorted to the point he decided to go on the "Today" show and tell the world that he had it for four years and was taking meds all the time. I think this is bullshit: I think Charlie had that shit, knew it, and because he was always high and had all that money, he didn't give a shit who knew or who he infected.

A part of the transformation that I am talking about is the role that money can play in this whole situation. As George Simmel (1978) made most clear in his work, *The Philosophy of Money*, money is not just capital or work, it is also "the ultimate confounding of things." It can make the small look big, the big appear small, the weak appear strong, and in the case of my own theory, it can make the traditional female and male roles look like their polar opposites. It can make the effeminate appear super-masculine and the white appear black and vice-versa. But it's not just the money: it's the manipulation of images that money can maintain that is making these "transformations" a reality.

In the previous example of young boys playing with Barbie dolls, that in itself is nothing wrong. I used to make paper men and women, cut them out and perform my own skits when I was young. What is important to note is that the media is reporting on all this and showing these photos of kids who appear to be gay and then presuming that any boy is alright in doing so. If a boy is playing with Barbie dolls, he's thinking about tits, pussy and all that stuff that comes along with a doll that is built to look like that. It's a part of the "transformation" that I am writing about, and it is most worthy of short- and long-term consideration and analysis.

Let me conclude with saying simply that I hope this book puts something on the minds of everyone who reads it. This nation (and the demi-gods who control it) is not above exterminating entire races of people, as it proved with the Native

American and tried to do with black people. It exploited thousands of Asians in the construction of the railroad system, and to this day harasses Latinos, having the nerve to label them, "illegal aliens." Black women, *who we say we love,* are in an endangered state, and it is up to us, as black men, to do something about it.

What I have written is an attempt to reject in detail, defiance and self-determination, the on-going lies that want the masses of people to believe that America is changing for the better when it comes to human relationships. In my view, this country is as neanderthal in its notions and asinine in its activity as it was in the 18th century, especially when it comes to male-female relationships.

The battle is against what is called "negationism," which is the denial of historic crimes. As one website source makes clear, "although the word is derived from the French term *négationnisme,* which means Holocaust denial, it can apply to other issues as well. One of those issues is the claim that black people sold themselves into slavery, that slavery was not all that bad, and worse off, that black men and women would be worse off had their ancestors remained in Africa. This is known in scholarly circles as "New World Negations."

Such negations are a key foundation that makes "the transformers" and their ranks continue to grow. This society is confused and in a constant of denial. That is why they are prone to radicalization, not because of influences from other countries or dissidents from overseas, but because of the kind of cultural confusion that the reality of "the transformers creates.

The "transformers," gradually changing social, sexual, psychological, legal and cultural roles, are weakening this nation, confusing the children and forcing adults to act in strange and aberrant ways. Many of the young people are rebelling because some of these transformations, which interfere with positive and productive child-rearing and family life, is just too much for many of them to bear. Turn on the television: people are "snapping" all over the nation, gunning down strangers and familiars as a way to cope with the kinds of "lifestyle alterations" that I have described in this book.

"Radicalization" simply means "to make radical, especially in politics." To act as if we don't know what the reasons for these anti-social actions are taking place is ridiculous. America was conceived in radical activity and this nation has glorified it and reveled in it. "We killed the Indians," "We put the blacks in slavery," and more recently, a president (George Bush) declared from the deck of a battleship in July of 2003, "bring it on." He had no idea that the people bringing it would be living within the boundaries of America. And so the "transformations" continued under the eyes and noses of an entire naïve public.

Can't you see it? George Clinton once sang that, "America eats its young." The world is watching. The people watching today are the grandchildren of the people that his nation bombed and beat up. Every other movie that hits the theatre is presenting someone from the Middle East as "an enemy." People are beginning to notice that America has the largest prison system in the world and that large numbers of those people are brown and black. And with gender role transformations going on, confusion permeates the thinking of a pacified American public.

America's priorities show its disdain for the non-white world. A man, Chris Kyle, who killed 160 people as a "sniper" has had a school named after him, Texas television pre-empting regular programming to show his funeral process (100 miles), has had a statue built and Bradley Cooper made a movie, "Sniper," paying homage to this murderer. What does this have to do with the transformations that I allege exist.

I have a theory about Kyle. He killed men from behind rocks and trees. The man who killed him was said to have mental problems. There were three men at the shooting range that day, although Kyle was married. This situation shows where Kyle's priorities were: he may have loved his wife but he was also obsessed with guns and killing. This means that he may have had mental issues, but America ignored that fact because he was a former soldier. And in like manner, America ignores other white people who they allow to buy guns, ammunition and the like.

These are the kinds of "exceptions" and neglectful activities that pave the way for the growth and expansion of "the transformers." If you can kill and serve, or if you have martially assimilated, then you can slip under the radar and engage in some of the behaviors I've outlined. If you're a black man you can wear diamond earrings and engage in downlow behavior. If you're a black woman you can scream, wear fake hair and take charge of a community and its children. If you're a white woman you can kick men in the nuts and call the shots for the system. And all this takes place because the same people who allowed and awarded Chris Kyle to do what he did are the same ones whose attentions are diverted while the "transformation" that I have described takes place.

While all this "transforming" is taking place, America is becoming a dictatorship and is violating the privacy rights of its own gullible citizens. Having become a debtor nation, this country is farming jobs out to other countries and raising college tuition; revising its history and working to eliminate its racist past from movies and old-time TV shows. The impact of the transformation that I have outlined cannot be overstated. America is so infected with all these internal problems and external enemies that even when it tries to do right it does wrong. The same people who have made decisions for centuries are still there in the guise of their progeny – progeny who, like their ancestors, believe in talking about equality while living in gated communities.

History shows two tendencies: that which rises and comes into power and then that which withers away and dies. America is in the latter stages and simply chooses to go out "in a blaze of glory" (ala Rome). The transformations that I have outlined in this book are but one example of the gradual deterioration of that great social experiment called "America." The National Rifle Association, the Tea Party movement, anti-immigrant hysteria (when white folks are the real illegal aliens) and the rise of a social networking movement that has people looking at i-pods as the world is crumbling around them – this is a sign of "the end of days."

Other than the five categories I've delved into in this book, there are other "transformations" that are worthy of observation and analysis as well. For instance, the Asian female is the new white woman on some levels, but most of them are sexual and social. She's quiet, "obedient" and by the white man's standards, she is no sexual threat; she is not slut-like like her white female counterpart who is so busy trying to adopt a masculine power role that she's denied that "sacred white womanhood" bullshit imposed on her by the white man.

The Asian woman loves that role and covets it. She cooks, she keeps her mouth shut, and physically she doesn't have "double D" size tits banging you across your forehead. She's small in stature which makes men with little dicks feel more confident. So check her out as her roles on television grow larger and she kung-fu's her way into the movie industry. They call her "exotic" because she has a little skin color and different eyes, but make no mistake about this: if she's in America it's just a matter of time before her power-made sluttishness begins to somersault her into lesbianism and power craving. The white woman may be the new white male, but this Asian bitch is going to be competing for "top dog" status as the new whore in American society.

The same can be said for these Pakistani women, and you are beginning to see it on the news reports. Keep track of that last name, "Patel," which is the middle eastern version of "Smith." They are gorgeous, have brown skin and long, thick black hair, which belongs to them – they don't have to buy it in hair shops. In fact, a lot of the hair that these black women are wearing belongs to these middle eastern chicks and their Indian (from India) counterparts. She has skin color, but she has Anglo facial features and she's sharp, just like that Asian chick.

The middle eastern male will join his Asian counterpart in one of two key roles in the media: (1) terrorist or (2) effeminate business man and sidekick. They're going to do to him what they did to Bruce Lee when "The Green Hornet" aired; Bruce was so great they had to suppress him by making him Britt Reid's valet. Reid had all the bitches and got the lion's share of the lines – all Bruce had was natural ability, and people tuned into see him, not a peckerwood in a plastic mask wearing a Fedora.

Another thing to remember: when it comes to the Japanese Asian, these white boys dropped two atomic bombs on them and forced them into "unconditional surrender." If you think these smart people who are students of history have forgotten this or are going to "let it slide" (the way we apparently did with slavery), then you've got another think coming. And already the Chinese are forcing America into debtor nation status by loaning them more than five trillion dollars. And remember: they are one-quarter of the world population and white folks are but a shriveling minority.

And that is why this demi-god spends hundreds of billions of dollars on movies that make him appear infallible, all knowing and omniscient. He risks the lives of directors, producers and actors creating situations where he will be looked upon in awe and deemed a truly "special" breed of man. He has actors spend months undergoing major body transfers so that they can become as muscular as possible (Kate Beckinsale, Jake Guyllenhall, Milla Jovovich, Terry Crews, Sylvester Stallone, Zoe Saldana, etc.) to make them appear far more in shape than most other people and promote and perpetuate the transformation that I allege is taking place.

From snow-laden mountain tops, burning hot deserts and deep underwater scenarios to other planets, futuristic settings and the re-writing of his history, this is a race (species?) with some serious feelings of inadequacy. So he will lie and spend all this money to perpetuate and distribute those lies to unwitting nations who are so starved for acceptance that they often doubt their own humanity.

And once again, I've put forth issues that nobody has the guts to verbalize. To recap: the white woman is the new white man (woMAN), the black woman is the new white woman and a "sister-dyke;" the black man is the new homosexual (masquerading as a "metro male"), and the white man is a self-appointed "demi-God. The homosexual, in general, is acting like (in terms of audacity and social protest), dressing like and being treated by a non-tolerant society as "the new nigga." Read it and weep.

My theory regarding "the transformers" is about preservation of the black race and taking advantage of the declining numbers of white folks. The concept of same-sex marriage is an idea that will expand the ranks of the transformers. People of the same sex cannot procreate at the same rate as they would under heterosexual circumstances and since most of them are white (black folks will imitate them and become more audaciously involved, no doubt) then that means less births. At the same time I am a supporter of adoption and these same-sex couples will be giving homes to kids who need parents. In many of these cases (depending on the age of the child being adopted), the kids will grow up confused and as a result, will expand the ranks of the transformers because of what sociologists will call "confused identity formation." Even now in September of 2015, Mira Loma High School in San Francisco, California has adopted "gender neutral" bathrooms for its students. There are more to come.

The white man has people going around talking about men who are friends having a "bro-mance." A bromance? What the fuck is that? Can't men be tight and be pals like we used to do without implying that they are romantically engaged? Do you have to pat another man on the ass, swap spit or date him in order to be a friend? The "faggotization" of the American male in general is epidemic and as I show in this book, the black man is the new gay (masquerading as what they call a "metro male").

But it's all over the place and it's crystal clear in the terminology these men use, the fact that they have to be within inches of each other's faces in order to communicate, their subtle hints and so on. And the world sees it and that's why the world doesn't fear this country despite it's huge military. A military of effeminate men and dykes is not going to scare anybody away; it's going to entice them to come on in, using subtle tactics, and then start tearing away at this nation from within.

As the Temptations would have put it, it's a "Ball of Confusion." And as a result, boys will date boys, girls will date girls and gays, in their fight for increased civil rights, will act like – and be treated like – niggas. The sister-dyke will try to raise black boys to be men and will fail – fags will be the result, hence feeding into the ranks of the effeminate black male ("metro male"). The white woMAN will teach her daughters to be more aggressive and in some cases, to see men for the assholes that they are. This will increase the ranks of the lesbian option and again, fewer births, more adoptions, and perhaps increased "hooking up" between the sister-dyke and the white woMAN. Confused? Trust me, so are they!

But the white man ain't confused. Even as I write these words in November of 2015, a Fox show called "Empire" is proving how confusing sex roles are and more importantly, it is black people who are being used to continue this "ball of confusion." The main character is "Cookie" (played by Taraji P. Henson) and her husband, a former jailbird who worked with her to found Empire Records. They are at each other's throats and divorced, they have a son who is gay and another one that loves white bitches. So the "transformer paradigm" that I've outlined herein is being addressed in all quarters.

When black people are pitted against one another, this takes the attention off of how fucked up white people are. Add that to the rumor and gossip mills that permeate American society and the world, and the black race, as we know it, has replaced the white man as the laughing stock of the universe. Mantan Moreland, Stepin Fetchit, Moms Mabley and Willie Best: eat your hearts out!

I'm no Christian, trust me. But I do believe this: "whom the gods would destroy, they first make mad." Look around you: the transformations I have outlined are responses to and examples of what some might call "mass insanity." And this nation and culture have only themselves to blame.

<u>REFERENCES</u>

DeNoon, D.J. & Smith, M.W. (2004, July 13). HIV's bisexual bridge to women: Risk posed by 'down low' men still unknown. *WebMD Health News.*

Dodge, B. (2008, September 23). Looking past the 'down low:' New research. http://www.eurekalert.org/pub_releases/2008-09/iu-lpt092208.php Johnson, J.B. (2005, May 1). Secret gay encounters of black men could be raising women's infection rate. *San Francisco Chronicle.*

Fletcher, Connie. (1990). *What cops know: Today's police tell the inside story of their work on America's streets.* New York: Pocket Books.

Hine, Darlene Clark, (2000, February 11). Struggling and surviving. *The Chronicle of Higher Education.*

McElroy, J. (2014, March 5). Ronda Rousey Says She Could Beat Floyd Mayweather in MMA Fight. Bleachreport.com. Retrieved from http://bleacherreport.com/articles/1981959-ronda-rousey-says-she-could-beat-floyd-mayweather.

Simmel, G. (1978). *The philosophy of money.* New York, New York: Routledge Classics.

Younge, G. (2004, April 6). Black women in US 23 times as likely to get AIDS virus. http://www.guardian.co.uk/world/2004/apr/06/aids.usa